M000033228

The Pillars of Confidence

THE PILLARS OF CONFIDENCE

Unlock Your Success
in Key Life Areas

TAMRA FAIRBROTHER GAINES

MILL CITY PRESS

Mill City Press, Inc.
555 Winderley Pl, Suite 225
Maitland, FL 32751
407.339.4217
www.millcitypress.net

© 2023 by Tamra Fairbrother Gaines

All rights reserved solely by the author. The author guarantees all contents are original and do not infringe upon the legal rights of any other person or work. No part of this book may be reproduced in any form without the permission of the author.

Due to the changing nature of the Internet, if there are any web addresses, links, or URLs included in this manuscript, these may have been altered and may no longer be accessible. The views and opinions shared in this book belong solely to the author and do not necessarily reflect those of the publisher. The publisher therefore disclaims responsibility for the views or opinions expressed within the work.

Paperback ISBN-13: 978-1-66286-214-4
Dust Jacket ISBN-13: 978-1-63413-543-6
Ebook ISBN-13: 978-1-63413-545-0

Dedication

This book is for every person whose inner voice has reflected negative thoughts but, through perseverance and understanding of core values, has overcome and created a stronger voice; for the people who choose to be warriors rather than victims.

My life has been shaped by the love of my family and the encouragement of my core circle of friends. I have confidence because of the role each of you has played in my life. Thank you most especially to my mother, Gloria Fairbrother; my sister, Shauna Brucker; and my brother, Kenneth Fairbrother, for making me strong from the inside out. And to my husband, Ron Gaines, you feed my soul and my heart daily. Thank you for your unwavering love and support.

[illegible] everyday person whose [illegible] negative [illegible] through perseverance and [illegible] care [illegible] and created [illegible] for the people who choose to be warm [illegible].

[illegible] life has been shaped by the kindness [illegible] and the encouragement of my core circle of friends, [illegible] because of the [illegible] each of you [illegible] my life, [illegible] especially [illegible] mother [illegible] father Simone Beckett and my brother, [illegible] for giving me strong [illegible] inside out [illegible] my husband [illegible] you [illegible] and my best [illegible] I thank you for your unwavering love and support.

Acknowledgments

I'm a firm believer that you are only as good as the people you surround yourself with. When people ask me what my greatest accomplishments are, I immediately think of the incredible relationships I have with my family and my friends. I can't think of a single person in my life (past or present) whom I cannot call on for assistance. Partly because I believe you should never burn bridges and partly because the people I have had in my life are so incredible, I would never allow a bridge to be burned.

Although the dedication to my friends and family is broad, this section of acknowledgments is specific to those who helped to shape the production of this book over the past two years. When I think about ethics and core values, I know I have learned lessons from those special people around me. Some mentors over the years have included Mary Kay Ash, Elyse Gut, Betty Garrett, Tim Parker, Bill Boyd, Karen Hart and Lynn Bjostad. Additionally, when I began this process, I immediately called mentor and friend Teresa Day to help. We held weekly writing sessions and quarterly weekend workshops for a year in order to get the book ready to send to the publishing company. Without her, my thoughts and ideas would still be in my head or on a sticky note. Her experience as the author of Toxic Clean Up (Morgan James, 2008) and an editor was a treasure to me, and I will forever appreciate her leadership and her friendship.

Years ago, I was blessed to be matched up to my Little Sister, Kelsie Cartin. She was and is an amazing young lady whose inner voice has expanded and flourished over the years. She is positive, strong, beautiful (inside and out), and a pillar in her own right. I have grown through knowing her, and she has been a blessing in my life. As the youngest in my own family, I'm thrilled to be her Big Sister.

In seeking a company to publish this book, I foremost wanted a company with a strong outer brand of integrity, with high moral standards. I wanted to find people I could trust to guide this amateur writer through a daunting process. Mark Levine and Brenda Rathje with Mill City Press and their entire team have been such people to me. Their tireless efforts to "get it right" with the design of the cover, the editing, and layout have been an incredible asset to me. Lastly, I believe we all can benefit from having a good coach in our lives. I've had several over the years in Rick Kolster, Melissa Brisbois and Judy Owen. They had such an influence on me that I became a certified coach as well to pay it forward to others as they journey this life with confidence.

www.tamragaines.com

Contents

Introduction

In 2008, I applied to the Big Brothers Big Sisters program, which pairs children with an adult mentor and friend. I felt drawn to this program, having no children of my own but a lot of love and friendship to share. Then, I was matched with a tall, beautiful, highly intelligent girl; however, she struggled with low self-esteem.

In cultivating this relationship and getting to know my Little Sister, I discovered that we were very much alike. During most of my own childhood and teen years, I also had very low self-esteem; so low, in fact, that I literally walked with my head down, looking at the ground. As I began to think about what had happened in my life that helped me develop into a confident woman, and more important, how I could share that information with my Little Sister, the thoughts for this book began to develop. It became my mission to help her see herself the way I saw her.

Researching the topic of confidence, I couldn't really find the information I was looking for. It was disappointing at first, but soon I realized I discovered a lot by working through my own memories and childhood issues. My earliest years were full of conflict; my parents separated seven times and had divorced twice by the time I was twelve. I was the spitting image of my mother and too often felt like I was the one in conflict with my father. I developed a behavior pattern of always trying to please him, but somehow I never could.

He would give me backhanded compliments such as, "You have such a pretty face, but . . ." or "You'd be so pretty if you'd just lose weight." I walked with my head down throughout my teen years. My father would say, "Lift up your head. Stop walking with your head down," and I just thought it was one more area in which I couldn't please him. I always felt alone, even when I wasn't. By the time I was twelve, I had even considered suicide as a way to escape the pain. My father clearly had relationship woes—he had five wives and was married seven times (twice to the same woman). My sixteenth year was a turning point for me. Dad had married an addict, and I was living with them, as my mom's job kept her traveling. I put together every bit of independence I could and moved out of my father's house and into an apartment with a friend. My core values kept me in school during this time and of course working to contribute to living expenses.

When I was a junior in high school, I enrolled in the work program and got a job at a State Farm Insurance office. I learned quickly—once someone showed me how to do something, I picked up on it right away. The people in the office were appreciative and complimentary. It was a good environment for me, and over the next few years, I began to gain confidence in my ability to succeed at something. I dressed professionally—not expensively but with clothes that made me look like a woman in business. I had gained the respect of those I worked with, and that acceptance began the foundation of building my confidence.

At the age of twenty-one, I became a Mary Kay Cosmetics consultant and earned a free car in my first year. I became a director in my second year. The Mary Kay culture is all about empowering women by recognizing and rewarding them for their efforts. I felt great, not only about what I had achieved but about the effort it took me to get there. During this three-year time period, I had the most profound change inside me, from the girl with her head hanging down to a confident young woman. I began to believe I could succeed in this positive environment. For the first time, I felt my success was not contingent on someone else's approval.

Then my world came crashing down, and my newfound confidence was severely tested. I did not have the people skills necessary to manage the continual rebuilding of my Mary Kay team, and my business dwindled to nothing. In the spring of 1995, I had to let go of the thing of which I was most proud—I turned in my car and relinquished my directorship. At the same time, I broke off an engagement with my fiancé, and my grandfather died. I had no job, no fiancé, and truly felt alone again.

This time, however, I knew I had a choice about the way I felt. My Mary Kay training took effect: "Everyone has a bad week; you can either let it define you, or you can get over it." I knew I could be sad for a very long time, or I could get my pity party over with and move on. This positive attitude really got me through this time without falling apart, and it increased my confidence in handling pressure and surviving.

I moved to Houston, where my mother was living, and started what became a fifteen-year career in the hospitality industry. The more knowledgeable I became in whatever I was doing, the more I earned recognition and reward, which in turn built my confidence and gave me the comfort to reach out and try new things. I began to understand that I could rely on my confidence to get me through when I still felt shaky on the inside. I could act as if I believed in me until I actually *did* believe in me. And it worked.

These are the memories and issues that came to me as I researched a way to help my Little Sister build *her* confidence. While I was searching for a way to communicate to her what I had found, I realized I had been forming my own ideas about growing in confidence. The basis of my thinking began with the understanding that God had made me and that I had a purpose in life. I might not be the most financially successful person, or have the highest title in my company, or drive the nicest car, but at my core, I have traits that make me a good person— traits that are not defined by circumstances. These traits are my core values—those things that matter most to me. I began to understand that acknowledging core values is where we must start the journey toward building more confidence.

Next, I started thinking about what would sabotage me along the way to building my confidence. Most often, I listen to my inner voice when it becomes critical of my character or actions. Our inner voice can so easily tear us down. I realized I had to find a way to turn this around, and use my inner voice to build me up.

My thoughts went next to how I present myself to others. Is what I feel on the inside portrayed on the outside? How do others see me? Am I portraying the image I want to portray with my attire, makeup and hair, and behavior? I call this my "outer brand."

As I continued to search for ways to encourage my Little Sister, I began to develop ideas around knowing who I am by determining my core values, being kind to myself with my inner voice, and then sharing that woman in the mirror with others by my presentation of who I am. These ideas have become my three pillars of building strong confidence: core values, inner voice, and outer brand. When these three pillars are strong, my confidence is strong. I believe these principles will work for my Little Sister, and for everyone who puts them into practice.

You *can* become more confident in your day-to-day life. You *can* become that confident leader, confident parent, and confident spouse, and the person that instills confidence in others. You *can* go on your journey through life with your head held high and look eagerly forward to a bright future.

> Keep your thoughts positive because your thoughts become your words. Keep your words positive because your words become your behaviors.
> Keep your behaviors positive because your behaviors become your habits. Keep your habits positive because your habits become your values. Keep your values positive because your values become your destiny.
>
> —Mahatma Gandhi

"If one advances confidently in the direction of his dreams and endeavors to live the life which he has imagined, he will meet with a success unexpected in common hours."

—Henry David Thoreau

CHAPTER 1

The Confidence Factor

Colton is an adorable three-year-old boy who knows that he can make his daddy laugh when he smiles his biggest smile and looks up, slanting his eyes to the right. Not only does this make his parents laugh, but they also like it enough to have him repeat it for family and visitors. Colton has also come to realize this smiling action can help him get out of trouble, so when he spills his orange juice and his dad starts to become upset, Colton smiles his very best smile and, with extra effort, slants his eyes to the right as far as he can, feeling confident that he can make Dad laugh. Colton is sure he can do it again, as he has many times before.

Dad catches the smile and the eyes and can't hold back his laughter. He is indeed more amused now, and Colton's *confidence* in his ability to make his dad laugh and avoid trouble is reinforced.

But there will come a day when Dad is no longer amused and distracted by this cute smiling action. On that day, Colton will put extra effort into the smile and the slanting eyes, wondering why the tried-and-true action is not getting the right result. His three-year-old brain will start to analyze the situation and make adjustments to his belief system about his ability to get himself out of trouble.

This example illustrates a process we all go through: what we *believe* about our abilities and ourselves sets the foundation for our everyday *actions*. Our beliefs come from our internal analysis of countless interactions, like Colton's, with our parents, siblings, teachers, friends, and other significant people in our childhoods. Through the years, we develop patterns of thought and action based on how we've made sense of it all. Our actions are simply the outward behavior of these inward thoughts and beliefs.

The modern school of thought called neuro-linguistic programming (NLP)[1] teaches that all human experience is produced by the combination of three components: the neurological system (neuro), how we use language (linguistic), and how we've programmed ourselves to relate to the world (programming).

NLP empowers individuals to break down the "programmed" parts of the thinking processes and to use language to re-create patterns for interpreting one's own actions and the actions of others. NLP teaches that once we have awareness of our belief systems and then alter the way we speak about and define those beliefs through language, we can actually *change the way we perceive our reality.*

NLP takes much of its foundational philosophy from early writers such as Napoleon Hill, who wrote the classic *Think and Grow Rich*. Hill was one of the first twentieth-century writers to explore the idea that our thoughts had the power to create reality. In 1937, he wrote, "Whatever the mind of man can conceive and believe, it can achieve." More recently, Denis Waitley, author, speaker, and motivational coach who has worked both with astronauts and Olympians, has tweaked the saying a bit for modern ears. He teaches, "What the mind can conceive, the body can achieve."

These principles are not just peppy motivational sayings—they are supported by neuroscience and brain research.[2] In fact, current science supports the idea that we can "rewire" our brains and thought processes, no matter what worldview and patterns we constructed as children. In other words, MRIs and brain research[3] now completely support Denis Waitley's claim that "what the mind can conceive, the body can achieve."

These breakthroughs in rewiring our thinking create exciting possibilities for increasing our confidence levels. By understanding that *we are the ones* who have created our own view of the world, and that it's possible to reprogram our view, we can tackle specific areas in our lives and gain greater confidence.

What Is Confidence, Anyway?

Confidence is the way we feel about our belief in our abilities and ourselves, either a low level of confidence or a high level of confidence. Our confidence levels are directly tied to the principles Waitley, Hill, and NLP have taught us: how we see (think about) the world and our place in it largely determines our degree of confidence in any given area. We know from experience that *feeling* confident helps us navigate through our lives with more boldness and a better sense of direction. Jim Rohn, arguably this century's great business philosopher, has said, "The greatest step toward accomplishment is self- confidence."[4]

In fact, confidence is the very thing that empowers individuals, groups, and even nations to stand against the crowd and go their own way. When Patrick Henry shouted, "Give me liberty, or give me death!" he was *confident* that living under British rule was worse than dying, fighting for freedom. When Neil Armstrong kissed his wife good-bye and boarded a mechanical spacecraft with about as much technological advancement as a VW bug, he was *confident* that he would step out of it onto the moon's surface.

The story of Olympic champion Wilma Rudolph is one of the most inspiring confidence stories of all time, because the obstacles this woman overcame were enormous. Infected with polio as a young child, her left leg and foot were paralyzed. She had to wear a brace and receive treatments to try to straighten this leg.

Wilma was born prematurely, weighing only 4.5 pounds, in 1940, long before preemie care became standard at hospitals. Like many children born before mass immunizations, Wilma also contracted whooping cough, chicken pox, measles, and scarlet fever. Handicapped and sickly, Wilma did not grow up in what we normally might consider an ideal champion- producing environment.

But Wilma's mother was passionately committed to seeing her daughter walk again. When Wilma made progress walking and playing basketball, her family built her confidence with encouragement and pride. By the time Wilma was twelve years old, she had joined the basketball team at her school, following after her sister. All of these circumstances, and Wilma's incredible natural talent, helped build her confidence level over time. In 1960, when Wilma stood at the starting line of her third race at the Rome Olympic Games having already won two gold medals, she was *confident* that she could win this race as well. Indeed, she did, becoming the first American woman to win three gold medals.

These few examples—and countless other examples you know—clearly show that high confidence has a place in world-changing events. High confidence also has a place in our daily lives. Most of us want to achieve something in our lives, whether it is a loving relationship, a better job, to set a good example for the kids, or any number of goals. Most of us also want to influence our families and communities for good. Having a high level of confidence helps us get there.

But how do we gain this confidence? How do we get more confidence, increase our confidence, and bolster our confidence? The following three-step process can help:

First, we need to understand who we are and what we believe our purpose to be, and determine what really matters to us. We need to understand how we view the world, and whether any of those views need to be altered by changing the way we think. This is called "settling our core values."

Second, we need to tune in and listen to our inner voices—the ways in which we talk to ourselves. Waitley's saying, "What the mind can conceive, the body can achieve," has multiple applications to our inner voices. When our minds are full of inner voices that discourage us and persuade us to give up our dreams, we need to learn to turn them into voices of support and encouragement. Changing the way we talk to ourselves is a critical part of gaining confidence in our lives.

Third, we need to make sure we are portraying on the outside what we want to feel on the inside. Our actions, attitudes, and even our attire are all connected to the way we feel about ourselves internally. We can limit our ability to reach our dreams if we don't pay attention to this aspect of our lives. This is called our "outer brand."

Each of these concepts—core values, inner voice, and outer brand—is a source of stability that supports our confidence, like three pillars that support a tablet:

When each of the three pillars is stable and balanced, our confidence rests securely on top. In other words, our confidence level *is a result* of the condition of the pillars. If one (or more) of the pillars is in need of repair, our confidence can become shaky and unstable.

While each pillar is its own source of stability for our confidence, each one also is dependent on the others. Gaps or damage in the first pillar will affect the other two, and gaps in the second pillar will affect the first and third pillar. For this reason, we will explore each pillar separately, as well as the entire structure as a whole.

The Foundational Confidence Principle

The factors that contribute to our confidence levels entered our lives at the same time we entered the world. Our family structures and relationships, our early experiences (like Colton's), our personalities, and our view of the world around us all helped construct our three pillars and whatever level of confidence we have today.

If we think back to our earliest memories, we can find significant clues about our early confidence levels. Remembering how we *felt* during the memory and what was going on around us also will help us discover what repair work we might need on the three pillars.

We will explore the meaning and effects of each of these pillars in the following chapters. We also will take an assessment to find our own confidence level, and develop an action plan to improve the level. Going through life with low confidence makes daily living much more difficult—we are more likely to approach life's tasks with doubt and fear. Or we may act in a manner that contradicts our core values and feel uncomfortable with the disharmony it creates. These feelings contribute to the overall instability of our confidence, and if left unchecked and unaddressed, it can lead to our confidence taking a severe tumble. Each time our confidence topples and falls and we hit the ground, we further damage our confidence and the pillars it rests upon.

The Six Key Life Areas

After we explore the three pillars and how they affect our confidence levels, we'll look more specifically into various parts of our lives. By dividing up life's circumstances into a handful of areas, we can isolate confidence problems and use specific strategies to increase our confidence level in a manageable piece of our lives. These manageable pieces are "key life areas."

- **Relational**: Covering anyone with whom we maintain a relationship, this area includes a significant other, spouse, children, siblings, parents, extended family, coworkers, colleagues, and friends. It also includes the one person most left off the relational list: *yourself*!

- **Physical**: This area covers the aspects of our individual bodies that can be poked, prodded, and measured—our weight, blood pressure, glucose counts, clothing size, and all the habits or lack of habits that impact these factors, such as our diet and exercise routines. It will also include a look at disease and general well-being.

- **Spiritual**: The term explores concepts of the greater world that are outside ourselves and ideas, bigger than each of us individually—from prayer to a higher being, meditation, and a reaching for something more meaningful than the physical world.

- **Financial**: This term pertains to the management of our funds. Do we spend more than we make? Do we save? Do we give to charity? Do we have financial plans, or do we live paycheck to paycheck? What does our financial future look like?

- **Professional**: This area covers what we do to earn money, whether we "play well with others"—our relationships at work—and our professional image. Do we have a passion for what we do? Are we moving forward?

- **Emotional**: All those aspects of our individual bodies that cannot be measured—our mental state, our feelings of love and attachment to other people, our feelings about the world and our place in it are covered in this area.

All Confidence, All the Time?

Having a high confidence level does not mean that we will be 100 percent confident, 100 percent of the time. First of all, high confidence is something we develop over the journey of life, which means there are times we are not as confident as we could be or would like to be.

Second, developing confidence throughout our lives comes not only from the support and feedback of others but also from understanding our own abilities and the best way to use them. Those times when we relied on our ability and we reached our goals in the past give us faith during the times of self-doubt. Consequently, we can rise above the self-doubt instead of being drowned by it.

Our level of confidence can ebb and flow like the tides at various times in our lives. Stressful events, such as divorce, work pressures, lay-offs, or family struggles, can leave us floundering in a sea of doubt and fear. It is precisely during these times that we can draw upon our past successes and come confidently back to shore on the rising tide. We can draw upon our past successful actions to lessen our troubles and solve our problems successfully. Going through this process over and over is what gives us further confidence that we'll make it.

Life, Liberty, and the Pursuit of Happiness

The bottom line comes to this: what difference does it make? Confidence or not—how does this matter? Why should we care about the level of our confidence and whether or not we feel confident in those six key areas of our lives?

The answer is simple: living with low confidence causes us to miss out on the potential personal growth, life experiences, and stellar achievements that *could* be ours if we'd only focused some energy on raising our confidence.

Additionally, our confidence levels affect the other people in our lives, especially those closest to us. We can impact our own children, nieces and nephews, and other family members with either a positive model of high confidence or a negative model of low confidence. All of our actions have ripple effects upon others; we want to make those ripples count for something good.

Still wondering whether or not a pursuit of higher confidence is worth your time and effort? Consider that the confident risk-takers who established our nation felt strongly enough about the rights of individuals to live out their own destinies that they encoded the principles in the Declaration of Independence:

> We hold these truths to be self-evident, that all men are created equal, that they are endowed by their Creator with certain **unalienable Rights**, that among these are **Life, Liberty and the pursuit of Happiness.**

How remarkable that the founding principles of our nation also can be the founding principles of our own personal journey toward higher confidence. History has proven that living with a high confidence level improves not only our own lives but also the lives of others. I challenge us all to declare our own independence from the oppression of low confidence, and embrace world-changing possibilities.

CHAPTER NOTES

1. For more information on NLP, visit www.nlpu.com.

2. For a comprehensive explanation of NLP and related research, see Steve Andreas & Charles Faulkner (1994). *NLP: The New Technology of Achievement*. New York: William Morrow & Company.

3. Shawn Achor (2010). *The Happiness Advantage*. New York: Crown Publishing Group, 29–30.

4. Jim Rohn. "On Not Settling for Less," *The Classic Collection of Jim Rohn*. Produced in audio for SUCCESS CD, included in *SUCCESS* magazine, February 2010.

SIDEBARS/CALL OUTS:

What we *believe* about our abilities and ourselves sets the foundation for our everyday *actions*.

> "What the mind can conceive, the body can achieve."
>
> —Denis Waitley

> "The greatest step toward accomplishment is self-confidence."
>
> —Jim Rohn

"We don't see things as they are; we see them as we are."

—*Anais Nin*

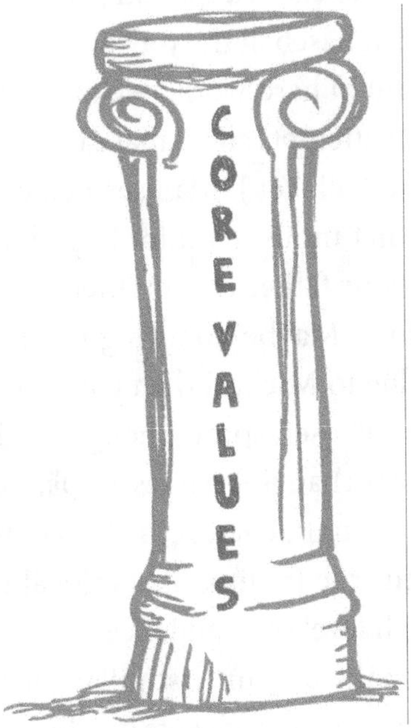

CHAPTER 2

Pillar: Core Values

Michael Jordan is, hands down, the very best basketball player on earth. During his career, he played basketball effortlessly, and his talent propelled and kept him at the forefront of his sport for years. Then suddenly, he retired, citing "personal reasons." Soon after, he took up professional baseball.

Rumor had it that his father, who had died, had always wanted him to play baseball, so he did.

As a baseball player, Jordan was still an exceptional athlete—good enough to claim a spot on a major league team. But he never excelled at baseball the way he so naturally did at basketball. No amount of hard work, pep talks, practice, "positive thinking," or other attempts could make him as good in baseball as he was in basketball. Yet Jordan seemed content to play out whatever it was that motivated him to pick up a baseball bat. Perhaps "honor your father and mother" was one of Michael Jordan's core values. Maybe honoring his father's dream was a deeper core value to Michael than continuing to be the best in the world at his chosen sport. Though we'll never know his personal reasons for changing games, he played each sport with a very high level of confidence, regardless of his personal stats. Michael remained true to himself, a critical part of acquiring and keeping a high level of confidence.

Core values make up our first pillar for this very reason: our values are the "bigger" concepts that lie behind our actions. Even when our actions might not make sense to the rest of the world, if they make sense internally, we'll be fine. Additionally, our core values can influence the second pillar, our inner voice and what it is telling us. Finally, it is in our outer brand, pillar three, where we display (or fail to display) how we feel about our values and what we say to ourselves. Our first pillar influences each following pillar, so core values is where we start.

What Is a Value, Anyway?

Perhaps the question, "What really matters?" was the very first conversation ever held. While we'll never know that, we know that philosophers and theologians have debated the questions of values for thousands of years, and the same debates go on today.[5] Whether or not our moral code is something we develop or something innate to human DNA, it is clear that our core values have an important role in determining the way we behave. In order to understand why we may have high or low confidence in given areas of our lives, we must start with understanding what's important to us.

We start by tuning in. In order to examine our core values pillar, we must *define* and *claim* our core set of values in order to live our lives with a high level of confidence. The beginning of the conversation about confidence—and the first pillar—is indeed settling the question of our own core value set.

We can understand which values hold the most meaning for us by picturing ourselves in a couple of different scenarios. First, picture yourself at the end of your life, possibly even at your own funeral. What do you want said about you on that day? Take a few minutes to write down some phrases. Now ask yourself, "Am I living my daily life in such a way that will cause others to say those things about me?"

You probably haven't included things on your list like, "She had great hair," or "He drove an amazing sports car." Most likely, the things on your list are values such as, "She was the kindest person I knew," or "His strength of character and self- discipline impressed me."

In the second scenario, picture yourself naked in a field. You have no material possessions, no circumstances, and no job, title, or salary. You are nobody's wife or mother or husband or father. You don't play golf or tennis. You don't make straight A's in school. *You are naked in a field.* Ask yourself, "Who am I now? Do I know myself? Am I happy? Am I proud of myself?

Do I even like myself? What do I still have here with me in this field?" You only have your values—those things that matter to you. Love, integrity, faith, passion, hope, kindness, forgiveness, gentleness, respect, wisdom, freedom, self-reliance, authenticity—which of these values defines you to your core?

It's possible that you are unsure which of these values are the most meaningful to you. In our extremely busy, technology-driven, never-alone-for-a-second lifestyle, you might not know yourself very well. Knowing who you *are* is knowing which core values best define you. You might need to spend a little time getting to know you. When was the last time you broke your word to someone? When was the last time you kept your word, even though it cost you a sacrifice? Your frequency in either breaking your word or keeping your word is a measure of your *integrity*, which must surely be on everyone's list of core values. The understanding of ourselves in relation to our thoughts and behaviors is not a new idea. In fact, it is one of the oldest ideas of human history, recorded in Proverbs 23:7. "For as he thinks within himself, so he is."[6] The ancient Greeks considered the axiom, "Know thyself," to be one of the most important issues a person could settle for himself. People have written about these ideas unceasingly for centuries. Shakespeare wrote, "To thine own self be true."[7] Jesuit priest Baltasar Gracian wrote, "Self-knowledge is the beginning of self-improvement."[8] British writer James Allen, author of "As a Man Thinketh," which inspired both Napoleon Hill and Denis Waitley, wrote, "All that a man achieves and all that he fails to achieve is the direct result of his own thoughts."[9]

Do you know yourself? Can you be true to yourself? If you need a refresher course on knowing yourself, then complete the following exercises. Start a notebook page with this question at the top: "What makes me great?" and begin to list all of the things that you are great at doing and feel great about being. When one page is filled, go on to another page. Never stop adding things you are doing and ways you are being to that list. If you truly can't come up with anything, ask a few close friends for help.

At the top of the next page, write, "What do I want people to say about me?" When people are talking about you, what do you want said? Probably not "She's such a gossip," or "You can't trust him with anything." So what *do* you want them to say? List all the phrases, acknowledgments, compliments, and affirmations you want to hear about yourself on this page.

At the top of another page write, "What do I have to do in order to hear those things said?" If you want people to know you as compassionate and generous, are you acting compassionately and doing generous things on a daily basis? If you want people to know you as an encourager, did you encourage anyone today? If you want people to know you as a person of faith, did you exercise your faith today?

Reflection on each of these three questions will help you get to know yourself on a deeper level and either discover or affirm those core values most important to you. Our core values define our belief systems, and our belief systems guide our lifestyle choices and behaviors. Before we can move on to building our confidence, we must understand those things that make us who and what we say we are.

Congruent Values and Behavior

Remember the term "congruency" from high school geometry? Two figures are congruent if they have the same shape and size. It is the same with our core value set and our outward behaviors. If they are congruent, this means our behaviors are the same shape and size as our values.

Another way to say this would be:

- When I act in a manner that *supports* the things I value, I am living according to my values.

- When I act in a manner that *contradicts* the things I value, I am living against my values.

When we hear a parent tell a child, "Do as I say, not as I do!" then we are hearing someone trying to justify the contradiction between her behavior and *what she says* are her values. This is also known as hypocrisy, and nobody admires or respects a hypocrite. Hypocrisy is the opposite of integrity, and other people will come to believe we either adhere the value of integrity or the lack of integrity (hypocrisy) by the way we keep our word or break or word—in commitments, in actions, in promises, and in behaviors.

When we profess to hold one value but act in ways that contradict what we profess to support, we actually damage this pillar, which in turn damages our confidence, and this affects our ability to live our best lives. In fact, behaving hypocritically is one of the surest ways to damage your self-esteem. You can't trust anyone, not even yourself!

These "incongruencies"—these fissures in the pillar of core values—are what create instability within this pillar. And when the pillar is unstable, the likelihood of our confidence becoming unstable is much greater.

When we are uncertain whether our values and our behaviors are congruent, focusing on the behaviors is the key. How we act is "telltale," which means our behavior is what tells the tale of our values, not the other way around. To say it another way, "Actions speak louder than words." This old- fashioned saying is the perfect test for determining whether or not we are acting as hypocrites. Focusing on our activity, those outward actions that we can see and measure, can help us define and claim our personal value set.

Define, Then Claim or Discard

Each value has its own merits and benefits. By definition, there are no immoral or harmful values, but is it necessary to hold all values in equal regard in our own lives? Not only is it unnecessary, but it's not really possible.

You may have inherited a primary value from your family or other influencers that you no longer consider your own primary value as you develop into an adult. You may have been raised to value family time around the dinner table, but with your hectic schedules and teenagers with jobs, you manage to eat dinner together only once or twice a week. You may have found your family responds best to a focus on monthly volunteering for the whole family. There is nothing wrong with having a different primary value set than your family or friends. It's really your responsibility to define your own value set and then live accordingly.

We may even become aware as we mature that behaviors we previously thought were good are actually in conflict with our core values. Many of us, for example, were raised in families that claimed the values of love and kindness, but the actual behaviors—such as a parent's alcoholism or verbal abuse—were completely incongruent to those values. Using our geometry example, the "shape" of love and kindness, and the "shape" of destructive alcoholism and verbal abuse are not the same.

Part of becoming a mature, stable, confident adult lies in defining our own value set, claiming those values we want to keep, and discarding those values or hypocritical behaviors associated with those values that we don't want to keep.

Core Values and Goal Setting

Going through the process of clarifying which values are most important to us also helps us get clarity on defining our purpose and settling our belief system into a larger plan for our lives. Too often, we get caught up in the short-term needs—paying the bills, providing for the kids, buying a new car, getting through the coming year, or some other short-term goal. We need to be able to pull back, take a deep breath, and visualize a larger future for ourselves. How? By setting goals and working toward them.

Goal setting is very important to the process of gaining and keeping a stable confidence. Peter Drucker (1909–2005), the economist and theorist credited with inventing the science of management, introduced the idea of SMART (**s**pecific, **m**easureable, **a**ttainable, **r**elevant, **t**ime-bound) goals back in the 1950s.[10] Drucker wrote extensively about setting goals in order to achieve objectives, with particular emphasis on taking the action necessary to actually accomplish the goal. He wrote, "Plans are only good intentions unless they immediately degenerate into hard work."

Let's review what each of the letters in SMART stands for and see why SMART goals work so well. First, our goals should be *specific*. If our goals are too broad, we won't ever know if we've attained them. For example, I might set a goal that says, "This year, I will be a better person." Being a better person might be a good idea, but it's not a specific goal that could ever be marked off as achieved. It's simply too broad. A great way to be more specific about our goals is to focus on the six key life areas (covered in chapters 6–10 of this book): relational, spiritual, physical, financial, professional, and emotional. Setting goals in each of these six areas gives us *specific* goals.

Next, there's ***measurable.*** Let's say we choose the physical as a key life area for our specific goal. If I say, "I want to jog more frequently," I haven't set a measurable goal. I have to quantify the goal with numbers: "I will jog one mile three times per week."

Attainable goals is a tricky one! We need to create goals for ourselves that we know we can reach, but we also need to stretch ourselves beyond our comfort zones in order to grow. Where is the balance? Again, the way to balance this aspect of goal setting is to know yourself. As stated earlier, we need to have a strong understanding of the reality of our gifts and talents, as well as the reality of our ability to access those gifts and talents, work them, and achieve our goals within our value set. If I were to set a goal to be the best basketball player on earth in a certain year, that, for me, would be simply foolish. But that is precisely the goal Michael Jordan set and achieved. A *relevant* goal is a very personal parameter. Only you know those things that are relevant to your inner self. Someone else may be critical of our goals, and we must learn not to let that criticism be a guiding factor for us. Can you imagine how many phone calls and e-mails Jordan received when his decision to play baseball became public? If he had allowed the criticism to change him, he would not have stayed true to himself.

Finally, we have *time-bound.* This simply means to put a timetable on our goals. Leaving them open-ended for the rest of eternity is a good way to squeeze out from under any commitment. Saying, "I will go to the gym three times per week sometime in the future" allows everything to become an excuse for not going. The bottom line of setting SMART goals is simply to put something in writing that we can know we've either reached or not reached. It's that simple.

Here are a few examples of excellent SMART goals:

- Beginning on January 26 until the end of the year, I will walk one mile, three times per week.

- Between June and December, I will read one spiritual book per month.

- Each month in this year, I will save 10 percent of my total income in a savings account.

Core Values and the Confidence Connection

In chapter 1, I defined high confidence as a *stable* confidence, one that is not easily shaken. Confidence is knowing what our abilities and circumstances make us capable of achieving. When we know ourselves, we know the things that matter most to us—our core values. Becoming clear about what matters to us creates a very stable source for our confidence to rest upon. Part of the process may involve reflection on what really matters to us as well as understanding our goals. Now that we've looked at how our core values can stabilize our confidence level, we'll move on to the second pillar, inner voice.

CHAPTER NOTES

5. http://www.nytimes.com/2008/01/13/ magazine/13Psychology-t.html?_r=1&ref=science. *New York Times* article "The Moral Instinct" by Stephen Pinker, January 13, 2008. Article examines whether we are born with a "universal moral" code as an innate part of human nature. Steven Pinker is the Johnstone Family Professor of Psychology at Harvard.

6. New American Standard Bible Translation (1960) by the Lockman Foundation. Published by Zondervan, Grand Rapids, MI.

7. *Hamlet*, William Shakespeare, Act I Scene 3, 78–82.

8. Gracian (1601–1658) was a Jesuit priest and prolific writer whose wisdom still appeals to a wide audience. This 1991 translation by Christopher Mauer (New York: Doubleday) has sold 200,000 copies.

9. James Allen (1864–1912) published "As a Man Thinketh" in 1903, and it has been considered the pioneering work of modern inspirational writing and thought.

10. Peter Drucker, *The Essential Drucker: The Best of Sixty Years of Peter Drucker's Essential Writings on Management.* Collins Business Essentials. 2001 New York: Harper Collins.

SIDEBARS/CALLOUTS:

Our values are the "bigger" concepts that lie behind our actions.

We must *define* and *claim* our core set of values in order to live our lives with a high level of confidence.

> "Plans are only good intentions unless they immediately degenerate into hard work."
>
> —Peter Drucker

"I think we all have a little voice inside us that will guide us ... if we shut out all the noise and clutter from our lives and listen to that voice, it will tell us the right thing to do."

—Christopher Reeve

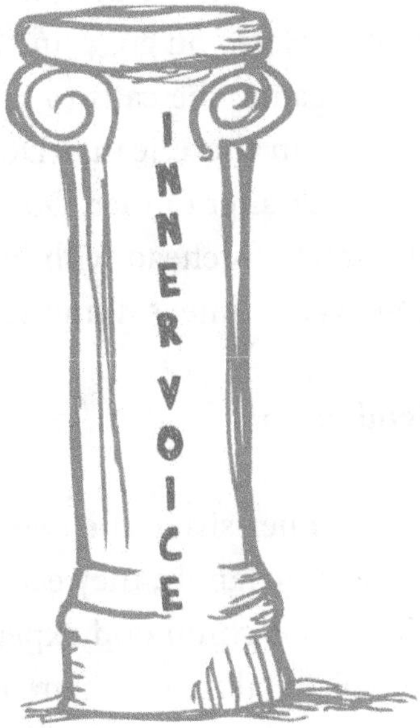

CHAPTER 3

Pillar: Inner Voice

Annie is a beautiful seven-year-old, with dark blonde curly hair hanging down her back and deep blue eyes as big as saucers. She is sweet and innocent and pays attention to everything going on around her, in order to figure out her world. Today, she's watching her father and older sister play basketball on the driveway. They are athletic and lean, and they play like this every weekend. Sometimes they throw her the ball, but they don't really want her to play. She's clumsy at dribbling and rarely makes a basket on the first try. Annie stays on the swing, eating a Pop-Tart.

Annie's mom comes out to the driveway, bringing her a sweetened juice drink. "Here you go, Annie," she says. When there is a break in the game, she calls to her husband. "Bill," she asks, "do I look fat in these jeans? Don and Susan are coming over to play cards after dinner. Do I look okay?"

Bill, wiping his sweaty forehead with his T-shirt, replies, "What? You look fine. What time is dinner?"

Inner Voice—Friend or Foe?

Although Annie and her sister, the two girls in the story above, grew up in the same family, they each internalized different messages from their childhood experiences and have very different inner voices talking to them now in adulthood. In the story, neither parent is trying to send a hidden message; it just happens. Our psychological makeup, our personalities, our birth order, our experiences, and who knows what else all contribute to the collective messages we hear and adopt as important in our childhoods. Those messages form the basis for the later internal tapes that replay in our brains.

Annie's sister grew up with inner voices emphasizing getting in the game, athleticism, and power. Annie grew up with inner voices emphasizing seeking outward approval focused on appearance, replaying her mom's insecurities over and over. Both young girls experienced issues with their inner voices in their later years. Once married, Annie's sister found it difficult not to compete with her husband, and Annie struggled with weight and eating issues. Both women also benefited from some of their inner voices. The sister had success with a career in the army, and Annie became a charismatic leader and public figure.

Inner voices can be positive or negative. Our inner voices can be most destructive when they prevent us from taking risks and achieving our goals in life. This is where most of us struggle with the negative messages that we have internalized since childhood. In fact, our inner voice tends to be full of the criticism of the *outer voices* in our lives. We may set a goal of taking painting lessons and hear our inner voice mutter, "Me? An artist? That's crazy." This voice may be a leftover reminder of corrections from a childhood that focused on practical activities rather than artistic endeavors. Your mother may have found you drawing instead of reading and burst out, "What on earth are you doing wasting time? Do something practical, for heaven's sake! You aren't artistic anyway."

We can't prevent our inner voices from developing or speaking to us as we go through our lives. We can't even predict what our inner voices will draw out of our past or project into our future. But it is never too late to get started on redirecting our inner voices to bring us encouragement and strength.

In order to accomplish this, we need to learn to hear, analyze, and manage our inner voices as adults. With a strong pillar of core values and an equally strong pillar of our inner voice, we are well on our way to getting and keeping a high level of confidence and a life of fulfillment.

First, Tune In

We often aren't consciously aware of what our inner voices are telling us. This can be true whether the voices are positive or negative, but since it is most often the negative inner voices that cause our confidence problems, we will spend some time exploring that. Why don't we hear them? Sometimes the volume knob is turned too low, and the negative inner comments just aren't loud enough to register in our brains. This doesn't mean, however, that the negative messages aren't harming us and our ability to succeed. Each negative message that our brain delivers to itself, whether we are consciously aware of it or not, destabilizes this pillar and therefore lowers our confidence level. We retrain our inner voice when we become aware of what we are saying to ourselves. Once we are aware, we can stop it.[11]

Awareness is the key to mastering the inner voice when it engages in negative self-talk. *Empowered awareness* is when we can hear the negative self-talk and interrupt it, and retrain our inner voice to be kind to ourselves. When something goes badly in your day, do you ever hear your inner voice saying, "Why are you surprised? Of course this happened to you today. Good things don't happen to you." Or perhaps you hear something like, "What an idiot! You just can't get it right, can you?"

When you hear your inner voice turning on you, put yourself in the shoes of the person your inner voice is criticizing, and turn that voice into a friend instead of a critic. Be a loving and nurturing force instead of a destructive force. Speak to that self as a counseling friend, and then, take your own advice. Turn your negative inner voice into your biggest fan.

Chelsea had been practicing for tryouts for the cheer squad at school. She knew the routines, and her mother constantly praised her for a job well done. After tryouts, however, the coach asked Chelsea to continue working on her cheers, saying maybe she could be on the squad another time. Initially heart-broken, Chelsea's inner voice told her she wasn't good enough and that she didn't try hard enough. Then, as if her mother were right there, she began to hear her words—the words of encouragement, of praise. Within moments Chelsea knew in her heart that she was good, and she began to feel better about her performance. She decided the coach must be having a bad day, and she would try again later.

Our inner voices represent how we *feel* about our talents and abilities. We should be giving ourselves messages that are:

- accurate assessments,
- based in reality, and
- based upon our abilities and talents.

However, our inner voice may not be "on our side" yet. It takes *active listening* to hear what our inner voices have been telling us. We may not even realize to what degree we already have an inner voice tearing us down. Denis Waitley has rightly said, "No voice has the power to discourage as your own voice, and none is as important as the one inside of you that says, 'Whoa, wait a minute. Stop, you're doing too well.'"[12] It is when we believe the voice inside our heads that we give up our own power and confidence.

How many little children do you know who are trapped by negative thinking? Not many! It's something we learn, most likely from our parents, but also from society, TV, our experiences, our teachers, and our peers. Most three-year-olds still view the world and its potential with wonder, and youngsters dream of being president, or an astronaut, or a professional ball player, or a rock star. They aren't yet aware of the statistics that say it won't be true, nor do they doubt their ability to do it.

Sadly, negative thinking and negative inner voices are learned—passed down to us by others and often by those closest to us. This is the main reason why it is so difficult to hear the negative inner voice and recognize its messages—we're comfortable with them.

If the negative inner voice is a part of the value set we grew up with and discussed in various ways at the breakfast or dinner table every day, we may have a hard time distinguishing it. Jim Will, PhD, the author of *The Power of Self-Talk,* writes, "Attitudes and opinions derive their power not from truth but from our belief in them."[13] When we turn the outer voices in our lives into our own inner voices, like Annie's mirroring her mother's weight concerns in the opening story, it becomes even more difficult to hear what's going on. This is precisely why it is so important to tune in and hear what we say to ourselves.

The Power of Our Inner Voice

Our inner voices have so much power over us because we give up that power to them. When we are willing to listen to a negative inner voice and believe the criticism, we help our inner critic beat us up. On the flip side, we can interrupt our negative inner voice and turn it into a force for good—our own good. What can our inner voices do *to* us? What can our inner voices do *for* us? Take a look at this chart:

Inner Voice can do **to** us:	Inner Voice can do **for** us:
Beat us up	Raise us up
Limit our contribution	Support our contribution
Keep us bound by fear	Give us courage to overcome fear
Sideline us in life	Give us the skills to play on the field
Return us to the start line in defeat	Help us take baby steps to our goal
How?	**How?**
Keep reminding us that we can't do what we want to do or think we'd like to try; each time we fumble, our inner voice says, "told you so," and eventually we quit trying	Keep reminding us that even though we are nervous and about to throw up, this fear is unreasonable and won't be strong enough to stop us from achieving what we want. This voice tells us "courage is feel- ing the fear and doing it any- way—go for it." Eventually, we overcome the fear and are able to lose the nervousness (or at least not let it stop us).

Facing our fears and pushing through to accomplish our goal in spite of our fears also builds tremendous confidence. It's a triumph to live through feeling uncomfortable in pursuit of a goal and, in the end, turn around and say, "Ha! I did it! I knew I could!" Our inner voice can be controlled and retrained to be our biggest fan and strongest supporter.

Childhood and the Inner Voice

Activity is what moves us forward. Giving ourselves a daily pep talk in front of the mirror has no value if we do not also take action. In fact, skip the pep talk altogether and get moving! Just like Dorothy in *The Wizard of Oz*, we walk around with the power to get ourselves where we want to go, but we get lost in asking everyone else what we should be doing.

We need to make time to think back and ask ourselves, "What did this little child want?" Most of us had dreams in our childhoods that weren't bound by any sense of reality. Make time to go back there and remember what it was you dreamed about, and see if you got derailed somewhere along the way. Take yourself back to your earliest memories, and answer the following questions:

1. What did I want?

2. What did I love to do?

3. Who did I want to be?

4. What were my daydreams?

5. What games did I play?

6. What happened to those dreams? Were they diminished by others?

7. What parts of those daydreams can I resurrect and bring into my life today?

When we were children, we often dreamed of goals that had no limitations whatsoever. Why am I suggesting we go back to that place? Because even if the activity involved in the dream itself may no longer be relevant or attainable, there is still much about that childhood state of freedom that can benefit us now. Take, for example, the young boy who dreamed of playing pro basketball, spending hours out on the court, perfecting his three-point shot so he could play like his idol, Michael Jordan. As a grown man, he only reached a height of five foot eight, and his talent level in basketball just didn't compete with the other young men in his high school or college.

What can he gain from remembering that dream? A lot! First of all, he had the abandon to have a big dream—this is a skill we give up as adults, believing it belongs only in childhood. Second, he mastered discipline and perseverance by practicing an element of the game for hours on end, knowing that its mastery was important to his success. This character trait is foundational to success in any endeavor. The ability to stick with something, persevering through practice after practice in order to better oneself, is once again a lifetime treasure. Third, by reflecting on this dream, he may remember how much pleasure physical activity brings him in his life, and he'll begin again to set goals that require strength and endurance, such as running a marathon or climbing a mountain.

Another benefit of taking our minds back to our childhood dreams is remembering to dream in the positive. Children don't burden themselves with negative realities— they don't consider statistics and probabilities. "I want to be the president," or "I want to be an astronaut," or "I want to cure cancer," or "I want to be a movie star." None of these "wants" has anything to do with probabilities. We need to relearn how to think in the positive.

Dr. Will provides a technique for creating a new picture of ourselves and focusing energy on that picture.[14] It begins, he says, with identifying what it is we want, instead of what it is we don't want. For instance, if I spend my time saying to myself, "I shouldn't be this weight. I must lose ten pounds. I can't fit in that dress," then I am spending all my energy on what I don't want.

Instead, I should create my new picture of myself and focus my energies on becoming that picture. I would turn around my self-talk and say things like, "I will feel great in a size 8 dress," or "I see myself moving more." This is a very strong example of turning a negative inner voice into a positive inner friend.

Inner Voice and the Confidence Connection

While chatting with a friend the other day, she referred to an incident in her day as "stupid." Her three-year-old overheard this word, forbidden in their home, and reminded her, "Mommy, don't say stupid. Stupid is a bad word." I have found, however, it is a favorite word of the bully in my head, who can't wait to tell me how "stupid" I am for taking a wrong turn, or forgetting some work papers, or any number of actions during my day.

We are often less kind to ourselves than we are to anyone else around us. If a colleague forgot something, I would never look her in the eye and say, "You are so stupid! Why do you always forget everything?" But I am perfectly willing to talk to myself in this terrible tone of voice. This is also true for many of you. The negative bully has to be conquered! Listen to the way you speak to yourself and to the tone of your inner voice. Replace negative accusations and critical remarks with positive encouragement and a little kindness to yourself.

Once we learn to interrupt the negative inner voice, we can change the course of our lives. Negative self-talk keeps us weighed down in the victim syndrome. ("Poor, poor, pitiful me.

My pants are a little tight, so I'm going to eat a doughnut. I feel sad today, so I am going shopping.") Our negative self-talk can be a driver to destructive behavior, and when we follow through and *engage* in the destructive behavior, our confidence comes crashing to the ground.

Instead of being a follower of a negative inner voice, become an empowered interrupter. This is one case where interrupting is not only encouraged, it's necessary to get yourself back on the right track.

Follow this process when you get trapped in negative self-talk:

- Listen
- Interrupt
- Talk back
- Make it your best effort

Everyone succumbs to a negative inner voice from time to time. In order to build your confidence, however, you have to develop an awareness of listening and really hearing what sorts of things you tell yourself about yourself. When you have awareness and a plan to overcome, you will not be victimized by a negative inner voice.

Being a gentle encourager strengthens this pillar and creates high stability for your confidence to rest upon. Take a moment to turn the negative voice into something positive by listing ten things for which you are grateful. I have shoes, I have a home, I get to eat lasagna for dinner, my favorite TV show comes on tonight, I got a compliment on the subway—whatever it is. Staying focused on things you can't control will only add stress and negativity to your life.

Now that we've looked at how our inner voices affect our confidence, it is time to move on to the third pillar, "outer brand."

CHAPTER NOTES

11. Matthew McKay and Patrick Fanning (2000) Oakland, CA: New Harbinger Publications. *Self-Esteem,* 3rd edition. Provides a systematic approach to identifying your inner critic and taking steps to silence it.

12. Dennis Waitley interview with Darren Hardy, SUCCESS CD, February 2010.

13. Jim Will, PhD, *The Power of Self-Talk* (2007). Houston, TX: Jim Will & Associates.

14. Ibid, p.70–71.

SIDEBARS/CALLOUTS:

Being a gentle encourager strengthens this pillar and creates high stability for our confidence to rest upon.

It is never too late to get started on redirecting our inner voices to bring us encouragement and strength.

> "Attitudes and opinions derive their power not from truth but from our belief in them."
>
> —Jim Will, PhD

"It is only at the first encounter that a face makes its full impression on us."

—Arthur Schopenhauer

CHAPTER 4

Pillar: Outer Brand

The third and last pillar that supports our confidence is our outer brand. Developing a personal brand is all the rage these days. If you perform a Google search on "personal brand," you' ll f ind hundreds of thousands of sites offering advice to you on how to brand yourself and what you offer to the world.

I believe your outer brand is a combination of your physical appearance and its level of correspondence with who you say you are. Outer brand is about matching your internal core, perceptions, profession, approach to life, ethics, and all your internal being to your outer physical presentation. Other people only have access to your internal core in one way, and that is by seeing and interacting with you. This "seeing and interacting" is the way other people experience you—your outer brand should reflect how you want to be seen and known.

When a company develops a brand, it paints a picture of the way it wants its customers to feel about the product. The brand presentation creates the magic around the product. A company might include the following steps in its brand development:

- Define the brand purpose.
- Align the brand features and benefits with the purpose.
- Create the brand presentation.
- Monitor brand relevance.

Let's take Coca-Cola, for example. Do you immediately hear "It's the real thing" in your mind? Do you see images of a magical world hidden inside the vending machine coming to life when a customer hits the Coke button? Whether or not you even like to drink Coke, the company has masterfully created a brand presentation that consistently represents to consumers a refreshing, magical, delightful drink that might just bring about world peace. That's how we "experience" the Coke brand.

How others react to the brand presentation gives us a good clue about the level of authenticity the brand holds in our minds. For most consumers, Coke is indeed a delightful drink. The brand presentation and the actual product are *harmonious.* Zappos is another brand that feels genuine and authentic to consumers. When Tony Hsieh, CEO of Zappos, entertains the media at his company's headquarters, he shows them around the office but also includes the bathroom, the water cooler, and his cube. Then, he invites them to walk around and speak to anyone at the office and to come back to his cube when they're done. Tony and his team work so hard at creating a culture at Zappos that reflects the company's core values that he isn't scared to turn journalists loose in there, confident that the company is living up to its stated values.

Oprah Winfrey has the trust and respect of millions of people. She often has been called the most powerful woman in the world. Her name has become synonymous with authenticity, integrity, and generosity. Her outer brand clearly expresses her core values.

When Target wanted to create a new brand image, the company leaders knew that had to show in their outer brand— the physical stores. Target wanted to shed its image as the place where no one wanted to be seen shopping and become a *destination,* a place people couldn't wait to get into. Target wanted consumers to view them differently than they had for years, but in order for that to happen, they had to make significant changes to their store appearance. The "new" Target has wider aisles, brighter lighting, well-designed graphics, and a new marketing strategy that showcase famous designers and their exclusive Target products. The transformation has been successful—Target has become chic.

What happens when a brand *is not* in harmony with its presentation? Everyone who comes in contact with the brand can feel it. This can be disastrous and embarrassing if you are a worldwide celebrity. The world wasn't surprised to learn that a pro golfer had an affair—but it was surprised to learn that it was Tiger Woods, whose outer brand presented a clean-cut family man and committed husband and father. He wasn't known as the carousing guy on the circuit. It was the *contrast* of what people expected from Tiger, based upon what he portrayed, that created the uproar.

The Goal of Your Outer Brand

In the case of outer brand, as I mean it here, perception *is* reality. How you appear, carry yourself, speak to others, and speak about others is all a portrayal of your outer brand.

The ultimate goal of your outer brand is to work the way every brand works: to create an impression of what matters to you and what you are promising to deliver. Other people cannot climb inside your head to know what you are offering; they can only look at what you put out there for them to see. Does your outer brand match up with who you are at your core and what you are trying to accomplish in life? It should all match and flow together and not create a discordant picture for others to untangle.

We've all heard the saying, "You never get a second chance to make a first impression." Research continues to support this idea—other people come to very quick conclusions about who we are when we are first introduced. Your outer brand is truly the only "statement" about you that some individuals will ever see. Princeton psychologists Janine Willis and Alexander Todorov conducted research that appeared in the July 2006 issue of *Psychological Science* that indicates it takes as little as one-tenth of a second for someone to form an impression of a stranger, and "that longer exposures don't significantly alter those impressions."[15]

Your inner voice represents how you perceive and talk to yourself; your outer brand represents how others perceive you by your presentation and actions. In order to have a strong pillar that offers solid support to your confidence, what you are on the inside and what you portray on the outside should match up. Peter Montoya, brand expert and author of *The Brand Called You*, tells his clients that they can double their business earnings by following these four factors:

1. Embracing the concept that shaping perceptions will bring business

2. Thoroughly integrating your personal brand throughout all aspects of your business and life

3. Consistently following up your efforts in marketing and communication

4. Supporting your brand promise with excellent customer service[16]

Outer brand is *not* about keeping up with the Joneses. Whether you are in an $80,000 house or an $800,000 house, who you say you are and who you appear to be either matches or it doesn't. Everyone has his or her own core values—you must be aware of them, define them, and be true to them. Outer brand is not about how much you can acquire or obtain; it is about being a true expression of your core identity.

The Business Side of Your Outer Brand

If your outer brand does not match what you promise to deliver in your professional work, you might be losing customers without even being aware of it.

Consider, for a moment, two women. The first woman is well dressed, her hair has been attended to, she is wearing a little makeup, and she is smiling. She holds a small briefcase or sample book in one hand and comes forward to greet you with a smile, and her other hand is extended for a warm handshake. The second woman is standing a little back from the first one. She is dressed in sweatpants with a stain on one knee and a T-shirt with a picture on the front. Her hair is in a ponytail, and she is not wearing makeup. She is actually frowning and looking at her feet. With no additional information, you must choose one of these two women to redecorate your bedroom. Which one would you choose?

The woman in sweatpants may actually be the better decorator, but she presents an outer brand that tells a different story. The client in this situation has her impressions of both women in less than one second, according to the research cited earlier in this chapter. Creating a great impression isn't about being pretty or handsome, either. A warm smile and handshake creates a better impression than an attractive face with a distant manner. In fact, a smile can be a gift at times. One particularly hectic day as I stopped in my car to pay a tollbooth operator, she smiled warmly and genuinely at me. It literally took me off guard, and I found myself smiling back. As I drove away, I felt better about everything in my day because she was willing to share a caring smile with me. Really, you have no idea how you might help someone during your day, simply by extending a smile and a sense of caring.

Although the physical appearance is important, your outer brand presentation doesn't stop there. What you present to others isn't just about how you look and what you wear; it is also about whether you represent your core values in how you treat people. You might be dressed up and looking like a million bucks, and that would make a good outer brand impression, but if you talk down to people every time you open your mouth, that would make a bad outer brand impression. In fact, your physical appearance could be stunning, but it can always be trumped if you are a terrible person inside that beautiful package. Bad-mouthing colleagues, gossiping, slandering, and focusing on the negative traits of others is actually a brand statement. You are offering information to your companions, and that information conveys who you are and what you believe.

The opposite is also true: you could be incredibly talented at what you do, but due to low confidence and an outer brand that doesn't match up to your talent level, nobody will ever know. If you are naturally shy, it may take more effort to engage other people in conversation. Just remember that they also have struggles with occasional inner voices, negative thinking, low confidence, and everything else you might occasionally feel, even if it doesn't show. So take that extra step of making eye contact, sharing a smile, and being sincere. You can truly lift someone's spirits and make a difference for him or her; at the same time, the effort will make a difference for *you*.

You'll remember I mentioned earlier that I used to walk with my head down all of the time—not some of the time; *all* of the time. When we lack confidence, when our confidence is very low and unstable, it shows in how we present ourselves.

Evaluate Your Outer Brand

Take some time to evaluate your current outer brand to see if you need to make changes to bring your presentation of yourself more in line with how you want to be perceived. Awareness is the first step. Once you become aware, you have the ability to make changes.

Oprah often talks about her admiration for Barbara Walters and the way she shaped Oprah's early career. "For the first six months I was on the air, I imitated her like crazy," said Oprah in 1987.[17] And why not? Barbara Walters exemplified in her outer brand everything that Oprah Winfrey wanted for herself: a caring interviewer who still got answers to the hard questions, a female anchor who earned the respect of her male peers, and a successful journalist who walked in doors that were shut to nearly everyone else. Oprah took Barbara as her example and imitated her style until she was confident enough in her own outer brand. This is a good pattern for everyone seeking to better their outer brand: find a great example in your field to emulate.

Once you identify that person, make a list of everything you "see" when you encounter this person. Make another list of the way this person makes you feel. Now compare yourself and your own outer brand to this person you admire. Make the comparison not for the purpose of feeling bad about yourself but simply as a way to expand your awareness. After all, you can't know what you don't know! You must expand your awareness (even if it is slightly painful) in order to make progress.

Another way to evaluate your current outer brand is to seek feedback from people you trust. Share with them your desire to match your internal core values and goals with your outer appearance, and ask them for feedback. Create a chart with three columns:

- Here's what I think I am portraying
- Here's my feedback from other people
- Here's ultimately what I want my clear outer brand to be

The above exercises are a way to break out of the limitations of your own viewpoint to get at the truth. The bottom line is that we want our outer brand to be a true reflection of how we want others to see us.

In sociology, this phenomenon is called Cooley's looking-glass self: we see ourselves as others wish us to be.

Make Small Changes

How do you eat an elephant? One bite at a time. This is the approach to take when making changes in your outer brand if it feels overwhelming. Go back to your journal where you've entered the three columns of what you think you are portraying, what feedback you are getting from others, and what you want your clear brand to be. Decide on two slight changes that you can make to your outer brand in order to bring it in line with what you want it to be. These two changes could be as simple as "do not wear sweatpants to meet new clients" or "don't swear in front of clients."

When you've conquered one small change, then you can begin another small change. In one year, it will be a year from now, and there's nothing any of us can do to stop that from happening. Time moves forward, even if we don't. If you make some slight changes in your outer brand, one year from now you will have made progress. If you don't, or if you keep procrastinating, one year from now you will be struggling with the same issues you are struggling with today. Is that where you want to be? The definition of insanity is doing the same thing over and over and expecting different results. To be changed, you must actually change.

Outer Brand and the Confidence Connection

Make sure your outer brand is sending the message you want sent to your friends, family, colleagues, clients, and everyone with whom you come in contact throughout your day. Having a positive outer brand in line with your core values helps to build your confidence, and it helps to still that negative inner voice. Each time you accomplish something meaningful to you, especially if it comes with positive feedback from others, your confidence can grow more and more. When any negative inner voices start chattering in your head, you can use the feedback others have given you to turn that negative chatter into positive cheerleading. Each time you present yourself and your outer brand successfully to others, you build up your confidence.

We've looked at how the three pillars of core values, inner voice, and outer brand function as sources of stability for our confidence level. When each pillar is strong, our confidence level is high and stable. Next, we are going to look at assessing our confidence level in six specific areas of our lives and the action plan for increasing our confidence.

CHAPTER NOTE

15. www.Psychologicalscience.org. Association for Psycho- logical Science. How Many Seconds to a First Impression? July 2006.

16. Peter Montoya and Tim Vandehey (2009) The Brand Called You. New York: McGraw-Hill, p. 32.

17. http://www.people.com/people/oprah_winfrey. Oprah Winfrey: Five Fun Facts.

SIDEBARS/CALLOUTS:

Outer brand is about matching your internal core, perceptions, profession, approach to life, ethics, and all your internal being to your outer physical presentation.

How you appear, carry yourself, speak to others, and speak about others is all a portrayal of your outer brand.

Outer brand is not about how much you can acquire or obtain; it is about being a true expression of your core identity.

"If you will change, everything will change for you."

—*Jim Rohn*

CHAPTER 5

Key Life Assessment

Now that we've explored the three pillars of core values, inner voice, and outer brand and have seen how each pillar contributes to the stability of our overall confidence, we will consider specific parts of our lives individually. I call these parts key life areas.

The goal of the following chapters is to isolate those areas in which we struggle the most with low confidence in order to create an action plan to turn around our feelings. After we've considered how the three pillars of core values, inner voice, and outer brand contribute to our level of confidence, we can create a pattern of setting and achieving goals. Each time we set and achieve a goal, we can support our confidence and grow stronger. We stay strong because in the setting and achieving of our goals, we actually change our behavior patterns and replace poor habits with better habits to keep the confidence we've worked to build.

When assessing yourself in each key life area, think about how satisfied you are with your life in this area, and whether or not this is an area of life you want to work on.

Use the following chart for a guide as you consider how to rate your confidence level in each area.

6	You have high confidence in this area. You have fulfilled your definition of success in this area. You are satisfied with your habits and behaviors in this area. When you consider this area, you don't think of things you need to work on.
5	You have somewhat high confidence in this area. You have come close to fulfilling your definition of success in this area. You are mostly satisfied with your habits and behaviors, though you can think of a couple of things you should work on.
4	You have some degree of confidence in this area. You haven't yet fulfilled your definition of success in this area. When you consider this area, you think of a few things you need to work on. Yes, you want to spend some time working in this area, but it's not pressing.
3	You have somewhat low confidence in this area. You're sure you *haven't* reached your definition of success in this area. There might be many things in the area of life that you need to work on.
2	You have very low confidence in this area. You might know where you want to be in this area, but you have been discouraged about changing this area of your life.
1	You have extremely low or no confidence in this area. In fact, you may not even be sure where to start. Thinking about it could even be overwhelming.

Don't be timid about rating yourself with a 6 in any area if you truly feel satisfied with your confidence level. Conversely, don't be afraid to rate yourself with a 1. The whole point of this exercise is to give yourself a starting point for building your confidence in one area at a time. When everything is in chaos, it's very difficult to find a starting point. Also, there is a lot of room for negative self-talk, which will decrease existing low confidence even further. When you work on these areas one or two at a time, you will gain more confidence by interrupting destructive behaviors more frequently, which will keep you on a positive path.

A final word of encouragement as you go through each of the next sections: Change is up to you; in fact, *only you* can improve your life. Don't hold back!

Personal Assessment

1. **On a scale of 1-6, how would you rate your OVERALL confidence level to <u>yourself</u>?**

1 2 3 4 5 6

2. **On a scale of 1-6, how would you rate your OVERALL confidence level to <u>others</u>?**

1 2 3 4 5 6

3. **On a scale of 1-6, rate your satisfaction of each key life area?** *Satisfaction is defined as content, confident, over-joyed and/or in control*

Spiritual	1 2 3 4 5 6
Physical	1 2 3 4 5 6
Relational	1 2 3 4 5 6
Emotional	1 2 3 4 5 6
Professional	1 2 3 4 5 6
Financial	1 2 3 4 5 6

4. **List two POSITIVE aspects about each <u>key life area</u> at this stage of your life**

Write the first thing that comes to mind, don't over analyze

Spiritual	____________	____________
Physical	____________	____________
Relational	____________	____________
Emotional	____________	____________

Professional ________________ ________________
Financial ________________ ________________

5. **List two NEGATIVE aspects about each <u>key life area</u> at this stage of your life**

Write the first thing that comes to mind, don't over analyze

Spiritual ________________ ________________
Physical ________________ ________________
Relational ________________ ________________
Emotional ________________ ________________
Professional ________________ ________________
Financial ________________ ________________

6. **Think back to your earliest memory as a child. How old were you?**

What do you remember?

____

____

____

____

____

____

7. **Think about the time between the ages of 6 – 10. What games did you play, how were you known to your friends or what interests did you have?**

____

____

____

____

____

8. **As an adult, do you carry any of the same interests or perceptions that you did between the ages of 6-10? If yes, give some examples**

____

____

____

____

____

9. **Looking back at question three, which key life areas did you rank a 4 or below?**

_____ Spiritual
_____ Physical
_____ Relational
_____ Emotional
_____ Professional
_____ Financial

10. Now, place those key life areas in order of importance to you at this time.

1. ____________________
2. ____________________
3. ____________________
4. ____________________
5. ____________________
6. ____________________

11. Is there another area that ranked above a 4 that you still want to place some effort toward improving? If so, list it below.

____

____

____

12. Now, re-rank those key life areas in order of importance to you at this time.

1. ____________________
2. ____________________
3. ____________________
4. ____________________
5. ____________________
6. ____________________

"Love comes when manipulation stops, when you think more about the other person than about his or her reactions to you."

—Dr. Joyce Brothers

CHAPTER 6

Key Life Area: Relational

The Relationships in Your Life

What exactly do I mean by the relationships in your life? To some degree, these are all of your connections to other people—your family, your friends, your acquaintances, your coworkers, your neighbors, your community at church or surrounding your hobbies, and anyone else you connect with throughout your day. Some of this even may extend to the strangers you encounter as they serve you in restaurants, at the bank, or in the checkout line, or even the other drivers on the road. It is, however, the relationships that are closest and most important to you that have the most influence and impact on your confidence level. We will consider those close relationships the most.

Multiple studies underscore the importance of building and keeping relationships in our lives, in order to stay healthy psychologically and even physically. These studies confirm that people who have good relationships and a strong social network actually live longer and have fewer health problems along the way. According to the Mayo Clinic, a "social support network" is made up of friends and family—those connections you build naturally through the course of your life.[18] By contrast, a social support system is not a support *group*—defined as a generally structured meeting with some sort of professional element. Though a support group can be very helpful in a particular arena, your social support network is not a "formal" or structured get-together but rather those moments and opportunities in which you spend time with people who matter to you.

Mayo also states that individuals benefit in specific ways from engaging with their social support network.[19] For example, we benefit by developing a sense of belonging, which particularly helps us avoid feeling isolated and alone in times of stress. Additionally, we benefit by achieving an increased sense of self-worth by knowing other people call us "friend" and that we deserve that title. And finally, we benefit by gaining a sense of comfort and security that we have access to information, advice, and guidance from other people we trust.

In our fast-paced times, it's not hard to live in an isolated fashion. Just ask yourself how many of your neighbors you know. How many of your neighbors do you even *see* on a daily or weekly basis? Apart from your work, do you have a community of people with whom you regularly meet? Even at work, do you have social encounters with your coworkers? You might be one of the many people who gets up each day, goes to work, comes home to make dinner and watch a little TV, and then goes to bed in order to get up the next day and do it all over again. Our very lifestyle can bring about a lack of relationships with other people.

You are less likely to suffer depression and anxiety if you have at least a few strong relationships. Atul Gawande, reporter for the *New Yorker*, wrote an article about isolation and the human psyche, noting, "We are social not just in the trivial sense that we like company and not just in the obvious sense that we each depend on others. We are social in a more elemental way: simply to exist as a normal human being requires interaction with other people."[20]

The article goes on to cover political prisoners held in solitary confinement and criminals in the US penal system, noting that destructive effects of isolation were common to both—deterioration of mental faculties, withdrawn behavior, disintegrating into a catatonic state, often including hallucinations and psychosis. Simply put, we are not made to survive alone; having good relationships is critical to maintaining a *healthy life*.

Some people who haven't been isolated but who have endured abusive childhoods or experienced trauma create a sort of self-imposed solitary confinement, cutting off other people from connecting on any level in order to protect themselves. Of course, this also prevents any deep relationships from forming, in the long run harming the individual.

Ultimately, only you can determine if your relationships provide you with the support that you need to remain healthy. In 1976, noted psychiatrist and professor at Brown University Sidney Cobb wrote a definition of "social support" that is widely used as a standard today: "Social support is defined as information leading the subject to believe that he is cared for and loved, esteemed, and a member of a network of mutual obligations."[21]

He went on to say that having a social support network such as this actually could protect people from illness and help them live longer. A study published in July 2010 by the University of Cambridge reports that having strong social support influenced health and death rates so significantly that relationship factors could be considered a major risk factor, like smoking or obesity.[22] Cobb's ideas were proven true, over and over again. Truly, the relationships we have in our lives can be a matter of life or death.

Reasons Why You Might Rate Yourself Low

Common issues in relationships that might cause low confidence can include developing an inappropriate dependency upon a partner, not understanding what it is you actually want from a relationship, allowing abusive behaviors to exist and survive, perpetuating abusive behaviors, having control issues, and not having skills in arguing and negotiating, among many, many others.

If you are experiencing some of these issues, you may have rated yourself with a score of 3 or below in this area. It's important to note that the *number* of relationships you have is not necessarily an indicator of the strength of those relationships.

Some people have a wide circle of friends but still may feel isolated and alone. Others may have few friends but feel richly supported and loved. Clearly, the number of people with whom you are involved isn't nearly as important as the quality of those relationships. Do you surround yourself with kind friends who support you emotionally in hard times, who help you discover your talents, and who cheer you on from the sidelines? Or are you surrounded with negative people who bring you down, focus only on themselves and what you can do for them, put down you and your efforts, and leave you feeling drained and empty? If you find yourself nodding in agreement to the second set of questions, you might also rate yourself low in the relational area.

If you find that throughout your life, you consistently end up with a group of friends or romantic relationships that are difficult, negative, or even abusive, it's time to take a deeper look at what your inner voices are telling you about relationships. Do your inner voices tell you that "all your romances will end badly," or that you "don't deserve friends that go out of their way to help you"? Take some time to listen to your inner voices on this topic and journal your thoughts. It is very likely that if you give yourself a very low confidence rating in this area, you have negative beliefs about what you deserve going on inside your head, and you may not realize it.

Additionally, your inner voices may have encouraged you to set poor boundary lines for the behavior you will endure in a relationship. People raised in emotionally harsh families generally marry into emotionally harsh relationships because they can't "hear" the language of scorn, ridicule, or put-downs.

Being raised in such an environment makes it familiar, even oddly comfortable. Here's a test to challenge you to see if you need to do journaling about appropriate boundaries: the next time you find yourself in a harsh argument with your partner, take time to objectively think through the scene. Would it be okay if your spouse were speaking that way to, say, your little sister? How about to your daughter or niece? Put someone else whom you love in your shoes and hear those words or tone of voice as spoken to him or her. Now how do you feel?

If this exercise made you defensive or angry on behalf of that person you love, then let it also make you defensive or angry for yourself. Just as you would want to stand up for that other individual, stand up for yourself, and reset your boundary line.

Finally, you might rate yourself low if you aren't currently in a romantic relationship. But this key life area is about all of your relationships and the basic ways in which you treat people and expect to be treated in return, not whether or not you are in a relationship.

Review some of your core values and see if you can find patterns in the way you think about your relationships and the core values that matter most to you. For example, trust, respect, intimacy, and commitment are all important elements when it comes to relationships. How do these values and others like them fit into your chosen core values? You might think that struggles in this area and struggles in another area don't have anything in common, but they actually might be symptoms of a larger issue with a core value or a negative inner voice.

Take some time to ask yourself these questions and journal your answers:

1. Do you have someone to call if you have an emergency?

2. Who do you talk to when you feel bad about something?

3. Does anyone ever tell you that he or she loves you and that you matter to that person?

4. Do you feel lonely?

These questions might be hard to answer if you are struggling with loneliness in your relationships. But take heart—you can have the confidence level you want to have in this area by making changes in the way you think and act toward others.

Recommendations to Build Your Confidence

The Golden Rule has been altered humorously to suggest many behaviors; for example, *Do unto others first, before they do unto you!* Such altered sayings are funny because we've either been treated in that manner, or we're guilty of treating someone else in that manner. But let's take the Golden Rule back to its pure truth: if we were to always treat other people the way we ourselves want to be treated, we would indeed raise our confidence in the relational area.

Treat other people the way you want to be treated. It's a simple statement that can solve nearly every problem in any relationship. Why don't we do it, then? Because it's often impossible to get our own egos and pride out of the way in order to get to the right behavior. We don't want others to treat us rudely, disrespectfully, or abusively, yet we can't seem to let go of the "right" to treat other people however our mood dictates. *I wouldn't have honked so loudly if you hadn't pulled in front of me. I wouldn't have snapped at you if you hadn't been so rude. I wouldn't have ignored you if you had been nice to me this morning.*

In the relationship area, it's so important to understand that we cannot change other people, but we can influence their actions. How? By knowing ourselves and drawing a line in the sand that sets appropriate boundaries between us and others. Here's a story to illustrate this principle:

A couple divorced, one key reason being the verbal abuse by the wife. After the divorce, she continued to verbally abuse her ex-husband whenever they had dealings with their daughter. As in the marriage, the ex-husband felt the ex-wife had unrealistic expectations about his role with the daughter. After several months, he finally stood his ground and said he wasn't going to take that from her anymore, and he laid down guidelines for their conversations concerning their child.

As time passed, he had to become assertive now and again to reinforce that he meant what he said, but largely, she changed the way she interacted with him. He was proud of himself for changing her.

Sometime later, after she remarried, everyone ended up together at the daughter's softball game. The new husband got exactly the same abusive and harsh verbal treatment that the ex-husband had borne while married to her and before he set the new ground rules. The former husband realized he had not changed her at all, but he had *influenced her behavior* by setting his own appropriate boundaries. When he refused to allow the rudeness to continue, she got better about her treatment of him. No, he could not change her—only she could do that—but he could influence the outcome by being clear about what *he* would put up with.

Keeping a journal where you record your "attitude of gratitude" toward the relationships in your life can really help you focus on the positive aspects of people. We live in a selfish world, where selfish behavior is lauded and approved—even worshipped, in celebrities. Sometimes it takes real effort to focus on *un*selfish behavior.

Here's another exercise that works particularly well if you are suffering from low confidence in the relational area. Start a section in your journal where you write down everything wonderful about you. I call it "what's great about me." People with low confidence can sometimes have a hard time imagining any positive qualities. If this is the case for you, then think about what *other people* compliment you for and have thanked you for. Continue to add to your list as people encourage you. One page will turn to two, and two will turn to three. Hopefully, you will come to understand the things that make you great and what you have to contribute to the lives of others. Make lists like this for your spouse and your children. The world is so negative. It's so important to encourage and support those things that make people great. Don't rag on them for their weaknesses and mistakes; instead, praise those qualities and behaviors you want to see most often.

Following is a short list of additional tips and ideas that can get you started down the path of building your confidence in the relational area:

- Understand what your gifts and talents are, and surround yourself with people who support you, not those who tear you down.

- Learn how to be a good communicator of your wants, needs, and dreams. Don't be afraid in your relationships to be clear about what you want and how you believe it can be accomplished between you and your partner.

- If you are single, be clear on what you want in your relationships. Make a list! Be as detailed as you want and include such things as stability, family, age range, spirituality, common interests. Along with the standard qualities such as integrity and financial stability, I look for the quality of relationships a man has in his life—his mother, his kids, even his ex-wife.

- If you are married, understand the strengths and weaknesses of each partner, and learn to work together within the *strengths*, instead of tearing each other down in your weaknesses.

- If you need to discuss a sensitive issue in a relationship, take some time to journal your thoughts and be clear about what you want to say. This practice can help you avoid losing your temper or getting off track and not covering the real issue. You'll be better able to appropriately articulate it to your partner.

Too often, we get caught up in a specific act that annoys us, like "he/she never helps me unload the dishwasher or clean up after dinner." Sticking on these details actually can derail the entire point that you would like to feel appreciated and valued. Try to stay with the root cause of your annoyance.

- Counseling can help. If you can't get the other person into counseling with you, then go by yourself until you can think clearly about the relationship.

Handling Difficult Conversations

When you know that you have to dig into an area and have a difficult conversation in a relationship, make sure that you pay attention to the time and place you start it. For example, don't try to begin a big conversation just as the other team intercepts the football, or right before dinner, or in any other inappropriate moment. In these cases, you are not "starting a conversation"; you are "interrupting," and it's not fair. Give your partner or friend or colleague the respect due a difficult conversation and only begin it when you both have the time to devote to the discussion, even if this means making an appointment with each other.

Set common ground rules, even if they are only for you. For example, be respectful, no matter what. Name-calling, accusations, "oh, you always ..." or "oh, you never ..."—these words and others like them only get us side-tracked into hurt feelings and do not solve problems. Some basic "rules of engagement" include:

- Try to see the other person's side.
- Make eye contact.
- Don't interrupt.
- Make "I" or "me" statements instead of "you."

Listening

Listening makes up the better part of communicating. If you can make yourself really listen to people, you will have happier and healthier relationships. Talk less, and listen more. Practice listening more in your relationships, even if you feel you don't need to. You might be surprised at the results.

The Caliber of Your Relationships

Remember the old Jackson Five lyric, *"One bad apple can spoil the whole bunch, girl"*? The people you surround yourself with will influence you. Are they "spoiling" you and bringing rottenness to your relationships? Or are they building you up and supporting you to be the best version of you that you can be?

Associate with people you look up to and who can influence you in a positive way, and stay away from those people who bring you down all the time. Your relationships should encourage and support you.

Action Plan

Relationships take time and effort. Be sure to put both time and effort into the relationships that matter to you. You cannot neglect and ignore people forever and then question why they've slipped away. Make the phone call, send the text, send the e-mail, or connect via social media. Technology makes it so easy. I have a friend whose teenage daughter was in a horrible state of rebellion and hatred toward her parents. Throughout this period, they texted her with short messages such as, "I love you anyway" and "One day you'll love me again." When she was ready to come out of that phase, their relationship was actually stronger because of the communication and continual reaching out from her parents.

If you realize that you need stronger social support in your life and are ready to commit to finding and making new relationships, here are some actions you can put in place that will help you meet other interesting people.

- Volunteer/become a mentor.
- Join a group.
- Pick up the phone and call an old friend.

After time has passed, maybe three to six months, rate yourself again in the relational area and compare your progress. Journal about it. Your journey will help you gain and keep a higher level of confidence in this area and in all the key life areas.

CHAPTER NOTES

18. Mayo Clinic: http://www.mayoclinic.com/health/social- support/SR00033
Social support: Tap this tool to combat stress by Mayo Clinic Staff.

19. Ibid.

20. "Hellhole" on March 30, 2009. (http://www.newyorker.com/reporting/2009/03/30/090330fa_fact_gawande).

21. Psychosomatic Medicine, September 1, 1976 vol. 38 no. 5 300-314 Sidney Cobb, "Social Support as a Moderator of Life Stress." Accessed at: http://www.psychosomatic-medi- cine.org/content/38/5/300.abstract.

22. Citation: J Holt-Lunstad, TB Smith, JB Layton (2010) Social Relationships and Mortality Risk: A Meta-Analytic Review. PLoS Med 7(7): e1000316. doi:10.1371/journal. pmed.1000316
http://news.byu.edu/archive08-Oct-touch.aspx.

"Those who think they have not time for bodily exercise will sooner or later have to find time for illness."

—*Edward Stanley*

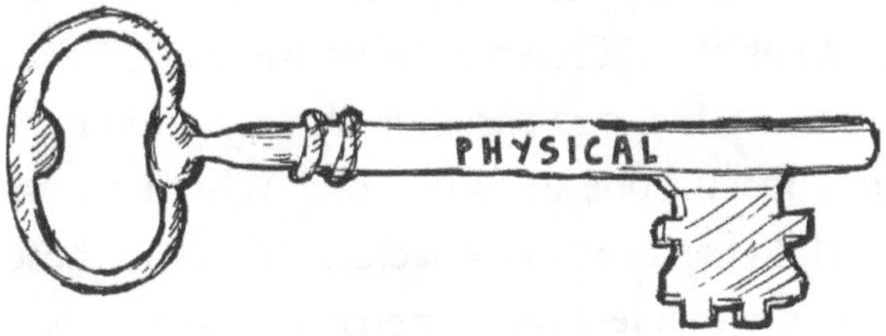

CHAPTER 7

Key Life Area: Physical

Your Physical State

What exactly do I mean by your physical state? Well, I'm talking very broadly about your health and well-being, not about whether you can compete in a swimsuit contest or body-building competition. Consider questions like these: Do you understand and apply healthy nutrition principles in your eating habits? What's your sugar consumption? Are you getting any exercise? How frequently do you eat fast food? When was the last time you ate something fresh from the ground or a tree?

The United States is the most technologically and medically advanced country in the world. People travel from across the globe to this country in order to receive medical treatment that's unavailable elsewhere. Yet according to statistics from the medical and health industries, US citizens are in the worst shape among countries in the world. Apparently, a life of ease is not actually good for our physical state.

It's hardest on the kids. The American Academy of Child & Adolescent Psychiatry (AACAP) has estimated that between 16 and 33 percent of children and teens are obese.[23] The AACAP also states that when one parent is obese, a child has a 50 percent chance of being obese in adulthood. When both parents are obese, the child has an 80 percent chance of being obese.[24] These experts also say that less than 1 percent of all obesity is caused by physical problems; more likely causes are poor eating trends, lack of exercise, family history and habits, stressful events, and life changes, as well as low self-esteem and depression.[25]

Obese does not refer to being overweight by a few pounds; it's being overweight to the point that significant health issues likely will develop, such as heart disease, diabetes, bone and joint pains, and even certain types of cancer, according to experts at the Duke University School of Medicine. These experts go on to say that death also should be included in the "health issues" brought on by obesity. In fact, they estimate that more than 400,000 annual deaths are attributable to obesity in the United States.[26]

It's surely a national crisis that up to 33 percent of our children are obese, limiting their chance of growing into lean and healthy adults. How have we declined into this state?

The way we live today has not been duplicated in the history of humanity. Never before have the masses been so physically *still*; never before have we controlled the temperature and the lighting sources, day and night and year-round. Never before has the majority of working people sat behind a desk or engaged in other mostly sedentary daily tasks. Prior to the Industrial

Revolution, people got an aerobic workout just by getting through their daily responsibilities. If they lived on a farm, they walked several miles in a day to get the chores done and animals fed. Even if they lived in the city, they were far more physically active, because there were no automobiles, no electric appliances—no freezer and fridge stuffed with ready food.

We now have excess time, excess food, and machines to make life cool when it's hot and warm when it's cold. And what has all this "advancement" brought us? It is literally killing us. Lack of activity destroys the good-health condition of every human being. This has been common knowledge for centuries, but somehow, in our twentieth- and twenty-first- century "advanced technological state," we have lost sight of it. Our bodies are not made for sitting still; like an uninhabited house, a mostly still body starts to fall apart. Additionally, when we sit still, we don't burn many calories. The natural result of lots of food and not much moving around is very poor health. We are able to lengthen lives through medication and surgical intervention, but we have largely failed to improve the *quality* of life for most people.

Too much food, with poor nutrition and not enough movement, also has facilitated a host of other diseases and chronic illnesses in Americans, including skyrocketing rates of diabetes and heart disease. The cycle is vicious and unrelenting—our lifestyle leads to illness, which leads to more illness. Illness and disease spin off into spiritual and emotional problems, which lead to more doctor visits and more medications, as well as more illness from side effects of the medication. The downward spiral of poor health and illness upon illness, along with a medical community that consistently treats only symptoms and not root causes, can create a great deal of confusion for people.

At the very least, we may find it difficult to determine the best course of action.

Reasons Why You Might Rate Yourself Low

You might have rated yourself with a score of three or below in this key area if you know you aren't eating well and exercising properly. The truth is, you know whether or not you are following the basic rules of health. You know by the way you feel each day. Do you feel fit? Do you feel healthy? Do you feel strong? If your answer is anything less than a resounding *yes*, then you have room for improvement in the physical key life area.

Another way to evaluate yourself is by considering your activity levels. For example, if you have a meeting one floor up, do you take the elevator or the stairs? Can you spend your Saturdays hiking or biking without taking a week for recovery? Can you garden for a couple of hours and feel strong? On the other hand, do you consider it a long-distance walk if you have to park on the outer rim of the parking lot at the mall? Your level of daily activity is full of clues to your physical state.

You also might have rated yourself low in this area if you are experiencing some of the symptoms of poor health, such as high blood pressure or fatigue, both very common among our population. And of course, you might have rated yourself low if you feel you are carrying excess weight, as most Americans are. You don't have to be overweight, however, to be in poor physical shape. In the United States (as in many Western developed nations), we don't suffer from a lack of food, but we suffer terribly from a lack of basic nutrition. You might actually look great in the mirror but feel terrible inside your skin. This could be another reason you might rate yourself low. Your body needs fuel (which comes in the form of calories) to function properly. The calories keep your brain working, your blood flowing through your body, your heart beating, and you maintaining a steady body temperature. Your body is an amazing machine, and it takes the calories it needs to do its work and stores the rest of them as fat for possible later use. However, in our modern day, "later use" never comes. There is no starving through the winter; nobody is pursuing you or chasing you out of your homeland. You have more food at your fingertips than you can consume and more convenience to get things done than anyone in human history.

Take a basic inventory of your eating habits. How many sodas do you drink per day or per week? How much alcohol do you drink? What's your intake of fast foods? Are you the sort of person who eats all your vegetables, as long as they're fried? Here's a good clue about your habits: if you get your meal at a drive-up window and can eat it in your car while you are driving, it's probably not good for you!

You might also rate yourself low if you are a smoker and know you need to quit. Awareness about the harmful effects of smoking has become so prevalent that no one can claim ignorance any longer. More and more public places, including entire college campuses, are declaring themselves "smoke-free" areas.

You might have negative inner voices challenging you about your fitness goals. Overeating is often a symptom of other unresolved issues—it is rarely about the food itself. Take time to listen to what your inner voices are telling you when you reach for certain foods. Take the time to write your feelings in your journal. You may come to recognize patterns in the way you feel and the types of foods you crave. Once you identify those patterns, you are already on your way to building your confidence in this area.

Recommendations to Build Your Confidence

Frankly, it *is* overwhelming to wade through all of the competing information about health and nutrition. Do diets work, or do they make the problem worse? Everyone seems to have a different opinion. Even if you do order something "healthy" at a restaurant, the chances are great that the portion is so large that you're overdoing the calories anyway. Fast-food restaurants offer "healthy" alternatives, but a salad loaded with a creamy dressing can have almost as many calories as a burger. And most of the available "quick" food at the grocery store contains chemicals and other additives that our bodies don't even recognize as food. Where in the world do we even begin to build our confidence in this key life area?

I recommend here, as in all parts of our lives, that we start with small steps that can move us forward in our goal to gaining confidence. We do know that physically fit people— those who pay attention to what they eat and make time to work up a sweat exercising on purpose—have fewer physical problems than those who eat whatever they please and don't move very much, so we'll consider this is a good starting point. We also know that moving around more has a positive impact on our mental state as well as our physical state. Dr. Daniel Landers of Arizona State University, in a report published in the President's Council on Physical Fitness, Sports & Nutrition Research Digest, concludes "there is now ample evidence that a definite relationship exists between exercise and improved mental health."[27]

The Unfortunate Truth about Our Physical Activity

In the physical key life area, as in all areas of our lives, having clear awareness of our reality is a first step to solving any problem. With our hectic schedules and time pressures, we might not even be aware of how much (or how little) we are moving during the day. We certainly are busy, but are we moving? There is a very simple way to find out. Attach a pedometer to your waist and count your steps. Many health experts use a daily goal of 10,000 steps as a good measure for achieving and maintaining a healthy weight. If you're like me, you are probably thinking, "I know I walk a lot during the day. I even park far away at the store and the office on purpose. I'll rack up those steps in no time." I was so surprised to see that I only took about 2,500 steps per day in my usual routine of leaving the house to go to work, coming home, attending to the household, and running a few errands. I was surprised this number of steps classifies me as "sedentary." In fact, 2,500 steps places me on the low, low end of sedentary. Consider the following chart, which shows the recommended number of steps for each category of steps per day:

<5,000 steps	sedentary (less than 2 miles per day)
5,000 – 7,499	low active (up to 3 or 4 miles per day)
7,500 – 9,999	somewhat active (up to 4 miles per day)
≥10,000	active (more than 4 or 5 miles per day)
≥12,500	highly active

None of us wants to think of ourselves as "sedentary"—to me, sedentary means practically immobile—but as I considered how I went about my day, the truth became too evident to ignore. Maybe your day is similar:

- From the bed to the shower (I am counting every step.) — 8
- Getting coffee, getting dressed, leaving the house — another dozen or so
- From the house to the car — 3 or 4 at the most
- From the car to the office — maybe 12, if I get there too late to park close
- Around the office — if I walk to the meeting upstairs instead of the elevator, and if I take the long way around to someone else's office — maybe 45
- Leaving the office to go back home —10–12 again
- Make dinner/collapse/watch TV — very few

Clearly, to get any higher than "basically immobile," I have to intentionally make time for exercising and moving.

The Unfortunate Truth about Calories

Next, let's look at basic calorie math. We all know that various foods are made up of different amounts of calories and that eating that food puts those calories in our bodies. Being alive (heart beating, blood moving, muscles working, lungs breathing) and moving (walking, running, reaching, stretching) removes calories from our bodies. When we take in *more calories* through our food than we use up by being alive and moving, we gain weight. When we take in *fewer calories* through our food than we use up, we lose weight. When the amounts are *equal*, we *maintain* the same weight.

The human body uses up about 2,000–2,200 calories each day just by being alive—with all the system metabolizing, lungs breathing, heart pumping, and blood moving. This is called the *basal metabolic rate*. It varies by person according to height and weight but is in the general 2,000–2,200 ballpark for nearly everyone. That's good news—we burn a lot of calories by being alive! The bad news, however, is that we generally consume *far more* than 2,000 calories per day; if this were not true, our nation would not be struggling with obesity. Grabbing a quick lunch of a burger and fries at any fast-food restaurant can load you up with more calories than you need for the *entire* day.

Here's where it gets confusing for most of us—we think that if we jog a mile or so, or hit the gym a few times, we can burn off those "extra" calories we ate with that doughnut for breakfast or those enchiladas for lunch. But even really strenuous exercise, like running, burns only about 200–300 calories per hour; walking only burns 100 calories per hour. If I want to lose a few pounds, but each day I eat more than 2,300 calories in my food, I won't lose weight, even if I walk a mile every day after work. How discouraging!

It's no wonder we get motivated to lose those pounds and then give up when we don't see results. We don't see results, because we aren't seeing our physical health from a clear enough viewpoint. We aren't considering the huge impact our modern-day living has upon our physical state. Let's take a moment to step back from the problem and consider some of the larger issues:

- Our bodies burn around 2,000 calories per day just living.
- The average American consumes more than 3,000 calories per day with large portions and processed, high-fat foods.
- Exercise burns about 100–200 calories per hour.
- The average American is basically sedentary, moving little during the day and not burning up those additional calories.

The only way to get and stay healthy in the physical key life area is to decide to be decidedly un-American in your approach to eating and exercising. It is virtually impossible to eat only 2,000 calories per day *unless* you modify the types of food you eat, from fast-food, processed, rich, and cheesy to fresh, whole-grain, and in smaller amounts. This is also precisely why "diets" don't work. If you drastically decrease the number of calories you consume for a time, but then go back to consuming them, you will gain back the weight. It's just math.

Knowledge is power; educate yourself on basic nutrition. Popular TV physician Mehmet Oz has written some of the most accessible, clear books on health. He also offers many helpful suggestions and important information on his television show and DVDs. Check them out—having a new perspective can motivate you to change your life. Sometimes all it takes for a person to radically change his or her lifestyle is just what you are doing—gaining knowledge.

Action Plan

The American Cancer Society now recommends intentional exercise for 30 minutes (preferably 45 to 60 minutes), five or more days per week.[28] You can include this exercise in your step count for the day. Numerous websites now allow you to track your steps online and set goals for long-term fitness. Perform a Google search on "10,000 Steps programs" to see hundreds of sites. Remember, your great-grandparents didn't really have to worry about adding excess movement into their daily routines, but *you* do.

The following list contains some of the food-related changes you can make in your lifestyle to help you gain confidence in the physical key life area. Read over the list and choose two items to start with today. Keep track of your progress in your journal.

1. Eat less sugar. Learn to eat fruits and vegetables as your sweet treats, with a little dark chocolate sprinkled in for variety. Food and taste buds are a funny thing— they have to be trained. Sugary snacks pretty much ruin you for enjoying the sweetness inherent in basic food. But once you switch over and consume mostly real food that is naturally sweet, and cut back on artificially sweet foods, like snack cakes, you likely won't miss them. Be prepared to take healthy food to work or school for lunch and snacks. Shop in advance, and have it on hand. Convenience is a very powerful motivator.

2. Learn to read labels. You'll begin to see the types of things to stay away from. All packaged foods have calorie counts on the label. When you are trying to reduce your calorie count just to 2,000, it helps to say no to a bag of chips—that's 450 calories in just a handful of chips, and it won't even fill you up or provide good nutrients for your body.

3. Don't crash cut your calories. Remember that your brain, your heart, and your cells do need calories to function. It's not wise to ever eat fewer than 1,500 calories per day, because you'll actually begin sending signals to your body that you are starving and in danger of dying, so your body will slow down the calorie-burning to conserve.

When you start filling your body with nutritious food instead of junk food, and you move your body as much as it was meant to be moved and used during the day, you will find yourself gaining confidence in this key life area. Remember, we're talking about *the rest of your life*, not the next two weeks before the class reunion or some other significant event that's coming up. Gaining and keeping true confidence in the physical key life area means nurturing and caring for your physical body over time, providing the right amount of balance between good food and exercise.

CHAPTER NOTES

23. "Obesity in Children and Teens," Facts for Families, No. 79, (updated May 2008). American Academy of Child and Adolescent Psychiatry, Washington DC. http:// www. aacap.org.

24. Ibid.

25. Ibid.

26. http://www.dukehealth.org. Care Guides: Understanding Obesity. "How Obesity Affects Your Health."

27. "The Influence of Exercise on Mental Health," by Daniel M. Landers, Arizona State University, originally published in series 2, number 12 of the PCPFS Research Digest, http://www.fitness.gov/mentalhealth.htm.

28. LH Kushi, T Byers, C Doyle, EV Bandera, M McCullough, A McTiernan, T Gansler, KS Andrews, MJ Thun, American Cancer Society 2006 Nutrition and Physical Activity Guidelines Advisory Committee. American Cancer Society Guidelines on Nutrition and Physical Activity for cancer prevention: reducing the risk of cancer with healthy food choices and physical activity. CA Cancer J Clin 2006 Sep–Oct;56(5):254-81; quiz 313–4.

"Just as the body cannot exist without blood, so the soul needs the matchless and pure strength of faith."

—Mahatma Gandhi

CHAPTER 8

Key Life Area: Spiritual

Your Spiritual State

Our spiritual state doesn't refer to what religious denomination you are affiliated with or what you do on Sunday mornings. I'm not talking about religion or specific religious practices. There are entire books on differences between denominations and the finer theological points, but this is not one of them. Think of this chapter as the "30,000 foot view"—an overview of sorts to help you understand your level of confidence in this area, and ideas on how to build that confidence in this particular area of your life.

It is good to believe in something bigger than yourself—a "higher power." For me, that is God. I'm also talking about understanding who you are in the universe and your purpose in the world. Do you feel at odds with a universe that is batting you around and playing jokes on you? Or can you find a higher purpose in your trials and suffering? Victor Frankl, an Austrian psychiatrist who was held prisoner for several years in Nazi concentration camps, wrote: "Man is not destroyed by suffering; he is destroyed by suffering without meaning." Finding spiritual meaning in life is a critical component of living a fully confident life.

One of the drawbacks of living during this technologically driven and fast-paced world is lack of time to spend in reflection and slow thoughts. We have managed to fill up every available minute of our days with images, sounds, activities, and obligations. In centuries past, every day had quiet opportunities to reflect—no TVs to watch until bedtime and no computers to surf while waiting to become sleepy. In fact, the world in general was a much quieter place, with far fewer distractions from yourself and your mind. We still have questions about the character and nature of God or a higher power and how we fit into his plans, but we have far fewer quiet moments to think through these issues. For most of us, spiritual reflection has gone down the same sad path as daydreaming—we just don't do it anymore. As a result, we may feel unsettled or unconfident in our spiritual life.

Reasons Why You Might Rate Yourself Low

You might rate yourself with a score of three or lower in the spiritual key life area for a variety of reasons. You might feel that you lack knowledge or theological training, and that not knowing the answers to biblical questions means that you should have a low score. You might feel that a lack of involvement in a church or community should rate a low score. You might be confused about what it is that you actually believe about God or a higher power, the world, and your place in it.

As is true in all of the key life areas, two people may have similar circumstances but rate themselves differently, based upon how those circumstances make them feel about their confidence levels. For example, take two women—Carol and Sue. Neither of them attends church on a regular basis. Carol has rated herself very low on the confidence scale because she feels she *should* attend church but is self-conscious about going alone. Her spouse won't go with her, and she feels that others may think, "Why is that woman here alone?" which makes her confidence level drop every Sunday morning, despite her good intentions. Sue, on the other hand, rarely attends a Sunday morning service but feels her relationship to God is extremely strong and personally deep. She rated herself high on the scale, confident in her faith.

Your rating will reflect how you view *yourself* in a spiritual context. If you are confident that you know who you are—a child of God created with a purpose to contribute to your own life and to the lives of others—you likely will rate yourself higher on the scale.

Think back to your first experiences in church and how they might have formed your perceptions of spirituality. Often, we develop an internal list of "shoulds" and "should nots." The list could include hundreds of items that don't even make a real difference but are cemented in our minds nonetheless; for example, you "should" dress up for church; you "shouldn't" go shopping on Sunday. Maybe you are rating yourself low because you are "should-ing" yourself to death. Everyone has an opinion of which church you should attend, what you should do and shouldn't do—how many of these come from God and how many are someone else's viewpoint?

You might be carrying around family baggage about spirituality that you inherited from your parents. Maybe Dad thought all ministers were thieves who found a legal way to get other people's money; maybe Mom dressed you up to show you off to other people, without regard to your spiritual state. Whatever the case, feeling confident in the spiritual key life area is an important part of having and living a confident life.

Recommendations to Build Your Confidence

I encourage you to pursue a spiritual path. Studies show people are healthier when they have a worldview that includes faith and spirituality. Drs. Harold Koenig, Dana King, and Verna Carson have compiled over 1,000 pages of research studies on the correlation between spirituality and health in *The Handbook of Religion and Health*, now in its second edition from Oxford University Press. The handbook reviews every research study completed on religion and health and happiness, from 1872 to 2010—an amazing 326 studies conducted all over the world. In nearly 80 percent of the studies, people who were more religious were found to be happier and healthier. Dr. Koenig, a practicing physician and professor at Duke University, writes, "the people in these studies did not become religious with the primary goal of becoming happier. I suspect that most became religious for religious reasons, and an unexpected side effect was that they became happier."[1]

A common obstacle for many in thinking about God or a higher power is the hypocritical living of others. Individuals who do not practice integrity in their values and actions, yet claim to be followers of God or believers in a higher power, can create stumbling blocks for those trying to seek a spiritual path. As discussed in chapter 2, "Pillar of Core Values," nobody admires or respects a hypocrite. Try to keep the behavior of others separate from your journey into spirituality, if it's keeping you away. A sense of faith and peace can help you remain confident when you might have become anxious in the past.

In fact, that sense of faith and peace in your spiritual life can truly make a difference in your everyday activities, especially when they are stressful. Tracy, for example, has been looking for a job again recently. The last time she changed jobs, the search itself produced enormous anxiety and stress. Not knowing what might happen—would she get a good job? Would she get any job at all? Would she remain unemployed for months?— interfered with her spiritual life and kept her from having any peace during the process. This time, however, she gained more confidence in her spiritual life by learning more about God and his plan for her life. This time around, she knows she is doing her best by seeking and going to interviews, but she is not as anxious with the process itself. She has gained confidence in her ability to trust God in the midst of the uncertainty.

Another way to gain confidence in your spiritual life is to practice forgiveness. Forgiveness is a critical practice because

---

[1] http://catholicexchange.com/2011/10/10/135704/, *The Catholic Ex- change*, "Bake the Cake before You Ice It," Dr. Harold Koenig, October 11, 2011.

without it, we allow bitterness to grow from anger, which produces all sorts of obstacles and pitfalls in our journey of life. Frederick Buechner, a Presbyterian minister who has written both highly praised fiction novels and spiritual essays over the last sixty years, describes the process of allowing anger to turn to bitterness in a most descriptive way:

> Of the Seven Deadly Sins, anger is possibly the most fun. To lick your wounds, to smack your lips over grievances long past ... to savor to the last toothsome morsel both the pain you are given and the pain you are giving back—in many ways it is a feast fit for a king. The chief drawback is that what you are wolfing down is yourself. The skeleton at the feast is you.

What a picture of the damage done to *ourselves* when we choose to hold on to anger and refuse to forgive others for their faults or their harmful actions against us. Forgiving someone who has hurt you doesn't mean you'll invite that person over for barbeque. It does mean, in your own spirit and soul, you let go of the anger you're generating because of the hurt or pain. It means attempting to get to a place where you can heal and move forward from the hurt. Journaling your thoughts and feelings during this time can be a huge help for processing your feelings, especially since feelings around hurt and pain can be intense.

If you are feeling like Carol—someone who feels like she should attend church but doesn't want to go alone—use the technology available to serve your needs. Many churches now post the Sunday sermon online. You can "visit" a particular church without leaving home. When you find the one right for you, you'll already be familiar with many aspects of the church to lessen the anxiety of that first Sunday.

If you are married to someone who doesn't share your faith or interest level, you might be frustrated about attending services or seeking out a Bible study. Consider, as Karen has, whether your expectation that your partner should "keep up" with you is realistic—or even fair. Karen used to feel exceedingly frustrated about "their" spiritual lives, until she realized that she was lumping her husband's spiritual experience into her own and that she wanted him to be exactly where she was in her journey. These expectations quickly became a source of conflict in their relationship, leading Karen to wisely reconsider her view of her own spirituality.

Karen came to the conclusion that she could only apply her expectations of her spirituality to herself, and she decided that her husband's role was one of support, not a mirror image of her journey. She decided that within her values, it was okay that he not accompany her to church each week, and (maybe even more important) she decided not to silently "punish" him for it during the week by making snide comments or withholding her affection from him.

As in the other key life areas, keeping a journal to explore your thoughts and feelings about your spirituality can be a huge help to building your confidence.

Action Plan

Many options exist for addressing spiritual confidence issues. Every bookstore has a religion section you can browse for theological or inspirational books. The Internet is loaded with good websites for daily reflection and study, ranging from brief segments to in-depth studies accomplished over a time period. You also can reach out to friends who are walking a spiritual path that you'd like to emulate.

As with most other reflective issues, our fast-paced and self-indulgent culture does not lend itself to the process of thinking about God. It's important that you carve out quiet time in your schedule for spiritual reflection. This could mean giving yourself a few minutes in the morning, taking out a book during your lunch hour, or creating time before bed. Only you know the best time; the critical element is that you *do* it.

Bookstores (and online stores) carry many types of Bibles. If you aren't sure which one to get, look for a daily devotional Bible, one that breaks up the books of the Bible into easy-to-read segments and offers some commentary or a short devotional with each day's reading.

Gaining and keeping confidence in the spiritual life area is a lifelong process, one that is meant to bring about peace in your spirit and soul.

"Act your wage."

—Dave Ramsey

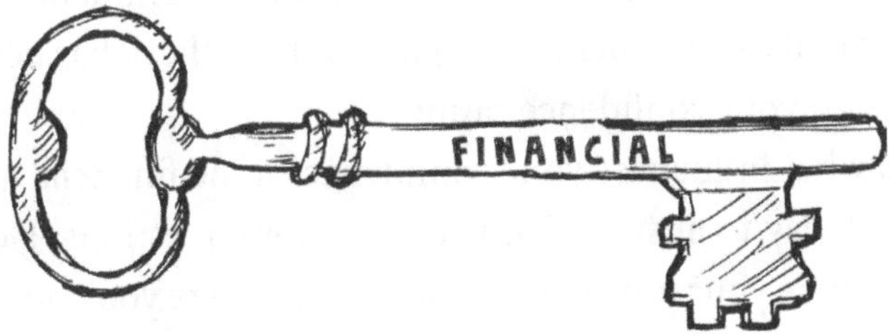

CHAPTER 9

Key Life Area: Financial

Your Financial Life

Your financial key life area refers to your income, your financial security, your financial freedom, and your future. It simply isn't possible to have a life and to function without some degree of financial means. Your particular financial means may exist anywhere within the range of very low to very high finances, depending on your values, life choices, background, education, family, or dozens of other factors. This chapter isn't concerned about what you do for a living or what your pay scale might be. In this chapter, the primary question isn't where are you getting your money, but once earned, what are you doing with it?

Interestingly, whether your finances are skimpy or abundant has nothing to do with your confidence level concerning those finances. You could be very wealthy but still lack confidence in the financial area. You could be living very modestly on a small income and be completely confident in this area (or high income and confident; low income and lack confidence). The point is that the number of zeros on your paycheck has nothing to do with your confidence rating.

So what influences your confidence in the financial arena? The best way to answer that is to ask more questions: Do you know where your money goes each month? Are you constantly running out of money before running out of month? Do you have money when emergencies strike, or can an unexpected car or appliance repair send you to the poorhouse? Are you looking over your shoulder, wondering what financial turmoil from the past might catch up to you?

Financial problems can disrupt every aspect of your life, including your most important relationships. It's important that we get our financial lives under control and that we manage them confidently, so that we are looking forward to a bright and exciting financial future, secure that we won't be straining family ties because of money.

Living in one of the richest countries in the world and having access to the highest standard of living in history can create multiple issues and complications for all of us. Our expectations of what constitutes a "normal" life are very different from past generations. Adults who came of age in the '80s and '90s might be the first general group whose parents and grandparents weren't scrimping pennies, living in modest housing, and rarely dining out. The world has changed in significant ways, thereby changing what each upcoming generation defines as an acceptable lifestyle.

Just look around. Elementary-school-aged children carry cell phones, restaurants are constantly packed, small families live in giant homes, cars come equipped as iPod- and GPS-ready, homes have multiple big-screen TVs, and new wardrobes are purchased each season. Most interesting, these items are not considered luxuries; instead, we consider them basic necessities, which is precisely the place where we get ourselves into financial trouble.

Dave Ramsey is an author, speaker, and radio host, offering practical advice and programs to people who want to gain control of their finances. He has a particular appeal as a tell-it- like-it-is kind of guy, with a large dose of humor and homespun wisdom. Ramsey tells his own financial story as a part of his program—a bankruptcy that led him to research how rich people stay rich. Ramsey has said of himself that he would do fine financially, except that he suffers from something called "stuff-itis," meaning that he wants to buy stuff! He's not the only one—it's a national epidemic.

Buying stuff wouldn't create pain for us if we all behaved according to Ramsey's command that opened this chapter: "Act your wage." There is the root problem.

Ramsey's quote is applicable to the way nearly everyone in America currently lives. If our jobs don't provide us with enough money to buy something we want (or an enlarged version of something we need, like food and shelter), our answer is to buy it anyway, on credit. Theoretically, this practice isn't evil in itself; what's derailing us—and thereby draining our confidence—is our lack of self-control in what we want and what we'll spend in interest to get it.

Our standard of living has a way of creeping up as our income increases. If and when we receive a raise or a bonus, most likely that money was spent in advance, and we once again are spending everything we make or more than we make.

Getting a grip on our finances really means getting a grip on ourselves and understanding the issues that motivate our spending. Once we understand why we spend the way we do, we can make lasting changes to our habits, and construct new behaviors that give us the financial freedom to pay our bills and take care of obligations—and have money left over to purchase the things we want, to travel, to give to causes, and to help family and friends.

If you rated yourself low in the financial key life area, it's an indicator that you've developed spending habits you must consider changing. Some of the action steps I am going to recommend are harder than others and take more mental discipline to implement. This chapter on finances and the chapter on the physical life are the two areas that require more dedication, discipline, and time to show results. Don't let this stop you. In order to keep a strong and stable confidence in your overall life, it's important to make progress in the financial area.

Reasons Why You Might Rate Yourself Low

You might rate yourself with a score of three or lower in the financial key life area for a variety of reasons. You might be living as most everyone else does—paycheck to paycheck, with no reserves in the bank and every dollar already spent before it arrives. If this is the case, even a small hiccup in the month—a flat tire, a broken washing machine, the need to visit a sick family member far away—can become an extreme emergency. Not only does this way of living your life have financial significance, it also can create enormous stress on relationships, marriages, and family ties, thus affecting and reducing your confidence in other areas of your life as well.

You might rate yourself low in this area if you feel you aren't living up to your own expectations or others' expectations of your material success. Maybe you think your house is too small or your car is too old, or you don't wear designer clothing or eat out at lunch every day. Handling the pressure generated from what other people believe about you or expect from you can be overwhelming.

Do you ignore the bills and refuse to look at your checking account balance out of fear? This practice could cause you to rate yourself low. Do you find yourself fighting with your partner over money? Are you facing more serious financial consequences, such as foreclosure or repossession? It's not uncommon. One neighborhood I know of in an upper-middle-class professional area currently has more foreclosures listed than it does homes for sale—it's an epidemic across the country. You might rate yourself low if you think you can't learn to handle money very well. Maybe the whole idea of balancing check-books and knowing your balances and debts is overwhelming to the point that you just ignore it. As in many things, we often have short-term vision when it comes to our finances. It's just so easy to spend money—that's basically the bottom line. It's hard to not spend money. We choose easy most of the time.

You might rate yourself low because it never occurred to you that there is a better way to manage your money until now. Everyone around us is spending more money on material goods than they earn in their paycheck—but that is not "normal."

Any of these reasons—or others—could be the cause of a low rating in this area. The good news is that you can absolutely make changes in your life to eradicate financial problems and to gain confidence in this key life area.

Recommendations to Build Your Confidence in the Financial Area

You are probably already familiar with the two best ways to curb your spending and understand your spending at the same time—use cash only and write down every expenditure you make for at least thirty days. As it turns out, ignoring the details is what allows us to pretend we aren't making a mistake on any given purchase. If I can't remember how much I've spent on purchasing coffee every morning, then I'll never have to reflect on the fact that the same $60–$75 could have paid a bill. Or if I can't remember how much I've spent buying lunch each day instead of brown-bagging it ($120 each month with a cheap $6 lunch), I don't have to think about how that money could pay for the car repair I'm going to need in the future, or go into a savings account for college or a vacation. Are you refusing to write down your expenditures because you might be scared by how much money you are burning through? That is a sure indicator that you need to write everything down.

Studies have shown that paying with a debit card or a credit card increases the amount a person is willing to pay for any item, as compared to paying with cash. Cash is real, tangible, and final. Swiping a card for a purchase is a lot like playing with fake money—it just doesn't feel real. Becoming aware of where your money is going is foundational to gaining confidence in this key life area.

What is your definition of a budget? Is it more of a suggestion or a guideline? Maybe the word budget has such negative connotations for you that you've never really looked into the process of developing one. Living within a budget is actually the only way to buy the things you want with freedom—living without a budget is what enslaves you. It's a paradox—the opposite seems it would be true, but it's not.

So the first step to gaining control of your finances is to get a realistic understanding of your actual spending on a daily basis. In other words, get out of denial. While you are journaling, look at your spending habits. How much are you spending for convenience? What are you buying that you could wait longer to purchase? Pay attention to where your money is going. Use your bank's online features, and monitor your money habits.

When I put myself on a cash-only basis, I became aware of my tendency to buy clothing—I thought of it as just picking up something new here and there. Using cash curbed this tendency so much that after a few weeks, a representative from my favorite store called me and said, "You're one of our best customers, and we haven't seen you for a while." That's when I truly realized the extent of my denial as to where my money was going.

Here are four money excuses that every one of us has used at some point—either consciously or unconsciously—to justify our spending habits.

1. "I have to live beyond my means. Everything is just so expensive."

2. "I don't know what to do financially. I didn't learn!"

3. "I had bad examples."

4. "I'm just going to buy a lottery ticket."

Making financial decisions with an excuse as the foundation is not a wise pattern of living, yet it's something of which we're all guilty. Now is the time to break free of excuses and gain confidence in this area. Take a deeper look into your spending habits and see if a different "truth" emerges.

What I'm saying	What I really mean
"I have to live beyond my means—everything is just so expensive."	I like to buy stuff! Don't bother me!
"I don't know what to do financially—I didn't learn."	I like buying stuff more than I want to learn how now.
"I had bad examples."	I don't want to exert the energy it will take to break these bad habits.
"I'm just going to buy a lottery ticket..."	I live in the future, which helps me avoid taking responsibility for the present.

So many resources exist in book form or on the Internet that it's really impossible to hide behind an excuse any longer. Dave Ramsey, the financial author mentioned earlier in this chapter, offers perhaps the simplest advice and easiest-to- understand program on tackling and subduing your financial problems—don't spend more money than you make, and put money away for a rainy day. As a nation, we have completely abandoned this common sense that our grandparents and great-grandparents lived by, because we have easy access to stuff—whatever stuff we might want—given to us by the use of credit. We will never become financially sound unless we put in place that most basic principle: *live on less than we earn.*

While technology has certainly made it easier for us to spend money, it's also made it easier for us to check ourselves and keep tabs on our spending through web-based programs such as ClearCheckbook.com and Mint.com. Give one of them a try for a month. They are free, and they just might save you thousands of your own dollars!

ClearCheckbook is free online personal finance software that has many features to manage your personal finances. You can see all transactions, balances, reminders, and notices on one page. You can create a "spending limit" to help you manage your personal budget and track all your spending with visual aids, like charts and graphs. Seeing a visual representation of where you are spending your money can be a powerful motivator for change.

Mint is free online personal finance software created by the makers of TurboTax. Mint's best feature is that you can't hide from yourself—it automatically updates your banking and credit card transactions, eliminating the possibility of "forgetting." The process is "read-only" so your secure data is not at risk. Mint automatically categorizes transactions as they are downloaded, and you can re-categorize each singular transaction to get a very clear picture of what you are spending. By using one of these online personal finance programs, you can gain a clear understanding of your monthly in-flow and out-flow of money. This is not rocket science. When you spend more money than you earn, you have financial problems. Gaining confidence in the financial key life area involves retraining your mind and changing your habits. Ramsey says, "A budget is telling your money where to go instead of wondering where it went." It's so easy to go through the week or the month using the debit card or using a credit card without a plan. A plan can make all the difference for your confidence to grow stronger. All this really takes is paying attention and a willingness to be responsible.

Following is a short list of additional tips and ideas that can get you started down the path of building your confidence in the financial area:

- Read a Dave Ramsey book on finances. If you don't want to purchase one, go to your local library, or visit his website: www.daveramsey.com. Ramsey has some of the most basic and impactful advice that can start working for you immediately.

- Consider all the various aspects of your lifestyle—the clothes you buy, the car you drive, the neighborhood you live in, the restaurants you dine in. Where are places you can modify your habits? You could consider a dramatic change, such as moving or driving a different model car in order to reduce your expenses.

- Know exactly how much money you earn every month, down to the penny. Know exactly how much money you spend every month, down to the penny. This is the only way to truly understand your spending habits.

- Do introspective thinking. Ask yourself the following questions (or some like them): Do I spend money to feel better about myself? Do I spend money because I don't plan in advance? Do I spend money because I don't have a concrete goal for my future? Journaling your answers will help you stay out of denial.

Action Plan

Understanding our true financial position is, of course, the first step to making it better. We won't know which action steps to take to improve the future if we don't know where we are in the present. The journaling system is the only way we can truly understand where our money is going. Once our spending history has been clearly identified, we'll know what steps we need to take to live within our means.

Also, it's important to forgive yourself and be patient. It will take time and discipline to reshape your thinking. You will be challenged every day by your old habits and the desire for convenience. That's okay! You can increase your confidence in this area by developing a plan and sticking to it. That sort of self-discipline will benefit you in every area of your life, not just in this area.

It is important to have strategies in place in order to support your plan. For example, if you've decided to brown-bag your lunch, then you need to plan to have the sort of food in your pantry you can actually take to work. Opening the freezer door in the morning and looking at a raw frozen chicken isn't going to get the job done. But when you are prepared for the challenges and then overcome them, you will feel empowered.

The fundamental problem is actually quite simple: in order to make a lasting change, you must change the way you behave. That may sound simple, but it's very difficult sometimes.

"If you follow your bliss, you put yourself on a kind of track, which has been there all the while waiting for you, and the life that you ought to be living is the one you are living."

—Joseph Campbell

CHAPTER 10

Key Life Area: Professional

Your Professional Life

Your professional key life area refers to your relationships at work, your professional image, your leadership style, your passion for what you do, and whether or not you are growing in your professional role. We aren't really talking about a specific profession or job title but rather your degree of happiness in that title, and more specifically, your confidence level in your professional life.

The point here isn't what your job is but rather if you feel confident and successful in it.

What is your definition of success in your professional life? Is it your pay rate, title, or promotion schedule? Is it your level of creative expression? Is it the degree of contribution? Is it your standard of customer service? Is it your series of awards and accomplishments? Discovering and then satisfying your definition of success in your professional life is more important than meeting a standard set by someone else.

As discussed in chapter 4, "Outer Brand," your physical appearance and how you present yourself to others can have a huge impact on whether or not you are comfortable in the professional key life area. Your professional appearance is the major part of your outer brand. Is it projecting the image you want for others? Remember that other people make snap judgments about us all the time—how we're dressed, how we move and conduct ourselves, and how we speak and interact with them.

It's important to understand that your professional appearance matters. I'm not talking about spending tons of money on designer-label clothing and accessories. I'm talking about taking the time to be neat, clean, and professionally dressed, creating an outward impression of the inner person you are (or want to be). Employers, potential customers, and others will make split-second decisions about whether they want to do business with you, based on your professional appearance.

If in doubt, follow the old-fashioned advice: be on time, stand up straight, look people directly in the eye, smile, and extend your hand for a firm handshake. Use a warm and friendly voice, and mind your manners.

Businessman and author Stedman Graham writes in his book, *You Can Make it Happen* (Simon & Schuster, 1997), that in order to achieve success, you must start with a vision. In order to have a vision, you must possess confidence (feel worthy of your vision), competence (have the knowledge, training, and skills necessary), and capability (feel capable of defining and controlling your own life).2 You can apply his principles to gaining confidence in the professional key life area. Think about your profession. Do you feel you deserve your position, have the training necessary to do it well, and feel capable of controlling your destiny?

For example, let's return to our two interior designers from chapter 4:

> Consider, for a moment, two women. The first woman is well dressed, her hair has been attended to, she is wearing a little makeup, and she is smiling. She holds a small briefcase or sample book in one hand and comes forward to greet you with a smile, and her other hand is extended for a warm handshake. The second woman is standing a little back from the first one. She is dressed in sweatpants with a stain on one knee and a T-shirt with a picture on the front. Her hair is in a ponytail, and she is not wearing makeup. She is actually frowning and looking at her feet. With no additional information, you must choose one of these two women to redecorate your bedroom. Which one would you choose?

The first woman definitely has a vision for herself as belonging in this profession and presenting an outward brand that speaks of confidence. She also has been trained and educated at one of the best interior design schools in the country.

---

[2] Stedman Graham. *You Can Make It Happen.* Simon & Schuster, New York, 1997. pp. 55–56.

She feels very capable of controlling the outcome of her professional life. She's a pretty good decorator, and if you hire her, you'll get a pretty room.

The second woman, poorly dressed for representing her field of creative design, might have a vision for success in her business, but she clearly feels undeserving of that vision. Her professional image and her feelings are at odds with one another, and because she has low self-confidence, her feelings of unworthiness win out over her professional image. She is not comfortable interacting with others, but she is an amazingly talented decorator who can provide you with not only a "pretty" room but a wonderfully delightful room, one in which you feel your own vision has been masterfully transformed. Sadly, her business flounders, even though she may have more talent than the first woman. We can clearly see how her low self-confidence affects her professional image, which affects her ability to engage customers and achieve a successful business.

Another part of the professional key life area is your satisfaction in the role you have. How do you feel on the drive in to your work? Do you look forward to your workday or dread it? Where would you rate your work-related stress level? If you spend the majority of your workday performing tasks you dislike or feel ill equipped to master, your stress level is likely to go through the roof and may spill over into other areas of your life.

If you are working for your paycheck but feel very disconnected from the daily job you are doing, you might need to reassess your core values and listen more intently to your inner voice. It is possible that you have chosen work that is in conflict with your core values. Go back through chapter 2 and journal through the exercises to find out what you value at your deepest center. Make a list of those values in a column in your journal.

In the next column, write down the various ways you feel before, during, and after your workday. You will likely find connecting points between the two. It is common to feel anxious, distressed, disengaged, and apathetic about your work when it is either not supporting your core values or going against them.

Curt Rosengren, career coach and author of *101 Ways to Get Wild about Work* (2007, Lulu Marketplace), writes that how you feel about your work can also affect your energy levels. He writes, "When what you do [in your career] is in alignment with who you are, you get energy from doing it. It's like water flowing along its natural riverbed. It actually gains energy from the path it's taking." Conversely, he says, your work also can drain you of energy if you are not passionate about it.

Reasons Why You Might Rate Yourself Low

You might rate yourself with a score of three or lower in the professional key life area for a variety of reasons. You might be unhappy in your job. Unhappiness at work can be caused by myriad factors. It's important to determine which factors are within your control and which factors are outside your control. Understanding this also can help remove the emotion from decisions you are making or might need to make.

Being unhappy at work could be a result of your own inner turmoil, which might mean focusing on the exercises discussed in chapter 2, "The Pillar of Core Values," in order to get to the root of the turmoil. You might not be able to affect the circumstances that are making you unhappy if, for instance, you have an unreasonable boss or are facing longer hours due to budget cutbacks.

You might rate yourself low if you are having difficulty in your relationships at work. This also might be a difficult arena because you might not have a choice about the team you are required to work with. Establishing appropriate boundaries can be important here. Consider your contribution to any problems. How are you making it better? Are there any ways in which you might be making it worse?

You might rate yourself low if you feel stalled at work. Maybe the work itself is not something for which you are best suited. Are you working in your strengths or in your areas of weakness? None of us is good at everything; we all are good at something. If creative expression is what makes you happy, but you spend eight hours a day crunching numbers on an Excel spreadsheet, you are likely to be miserable.

Are you allowing fear to block you from moving forward? Maybe you need additional training, schooling, or certification. Is something stopping you from pursuing that?

Recommendations to Build Your Confidence

The best recommendation for becoming and staying happy in your professional life is to know yourself. Understand your own passions. Understand what satisfies you on the deepest level and find a way to meet those desires in your workplace. After all, most people working in a job outside the home spend many more hours in pursuit of that paycheck than they do in other activities. If you are able to find work that pays you and that you enjoy and find value in, you are much more likely to be confident and happy in your professional life.

In an uncertain economy, it might not be feasible for you to make changes inside your workday. If this is the case, make some changes outside your workday to make things more bearable. Take the time to educate yourself with books, CDs, or other material, so that if an opportunity presents itself, you will be prepared to move forward.

Staying Positive in a Negative Environment

It can be difficult to stay positive in a negative work environment. Negative environments can be short term or long term. A short-term negative environment might be created during a high-pressure project that has a tight deadline. Once completed, the environment can return to a positive one. It's much more challenging to stay positive in an environment that is chronically negative. What can you do under these circumstances?

Strive to keep a positive attitude toward others. Avoid gossip and negative input about coworkers, even if you know something negative to be true. Negativity is like a downward spiral—once begun, it's difficult to stop and reverse, and good things get swept away with the bad.

Try to encourage positive conversation with colleagues. If that's not possible, then at least avoid the negative. If you have to work with an overly negative coworker, put up professional boundaries and do not be drawn into personal or negative conversations. Keep the focus on the task at hand and how best to accomplish it. If the entire workplace culture is negative, it's best to consider moving on to a new place. Chronic negativity increases stress and can make you miserable.

Listening may be the most important skill you can develop in the workplace to avoid misunderstandings and unnecessary drama. When a person feels that others are listening to him, he is much more likely to cooperate in problem solving.

Mine Your Company's Resources

Many companies have resources to support continuing education for employees or even options for supplementing tuition at school or other certification programs. If there is a specific training program offered in your area that you feel would benefit your employer, create a proposal for your boss, explaining how you could help the company by attending.

Expand Your Horizons

If your company doesn't offer resources for expanding your horizons, don't let that stop you. Thinking about a major career change can be extremely daunting, but if you are miserable in your professional life, it's worth considering. You might have chosen your line of work before you even knew what excited you about work. You might have grown into a different person who would have chosen a different line of work "back then." In today's world, we have so many more options for gaining skills and education because of technology. Do some research on going back to school, becoming certified in a new field, or develop a new path to chase a new dream.

Action Plan

It can be very scary to think about leaving the comfort and security of a job, even if that job is making you miserable. But you must ask yourself, "Am I willing to let fear prevent me from creating a better professional life for myself?" I hope this book can help you say no. Fear is a lack of confidence, and building your confidence is what this book is all about. As in all things, journaling can help you explore both your options and your fears, with no risk other than facing the possibilities. Put aside your fears, and play the *what if* game. Ask yourself, "What if I went back to school part-time? How much would it cost? How long would it take? What would I study?" Balance those answers against only daydreaming about how happy you would be in a professional career about which you could feel passionate.

It is critically important to acknowledge and keep appropriate boundaries in your life. Know what you will and will not put up with in the professional key life area. Ask yourself, "Do I stay or go? Do I find something more suited to me?" Journal about how the answers make you feel.

Below are a few questions to get you thinking about your professional key life area, and your confidence level concerning it. Ask yourself these questions and journal about the answers:

1. Do I feel optimistic when I think about my job over the next twelve months?

2. Do I feel like I am in charge of the important decisions I must make about my job and career? Do I feel as if someone else is in control of me?

3. On Monday mornings when I wake up to go to work, I feel ___. (complete the sentence)

4. Once at work, do I feel respected and valued by my coworkers and bosses? Do I respect and value my coworkers and bosses?

"Feelings or emotions are the universal language and are to be hon- ored. They are the authentic expression of who you are at your deepest place."

—Judith Wright

CHAPTER 11

Key Life Area: Emotional

Your Emotional Life

Emotions are defined as specific feelings, such as joy, grief, fear, anger, excitement, hatred, and love. Emotions often are accompanied by gestures or physical actions, such as laughing, blushing, clenching teeth or fists, or screaming. Emotions, however, do not need a physical expression to be deeply felt, for they are internal and can be experienced with no outward show at all.

Emotions can be intense—and tricky! Do we trust our emotions or deny them? Do we share them or hide them? Do our emotions cause us distress on a regular basis? Just as we mature physically and intellectually as we grow into adults, we also *should* mature emotionally, developing healthy strategies to cope with intense emotions. This doesn't always happen, though, causing us to enter adulthood with emotional immaturity issues. Lack of control over anger and using feelings to manipulate others are two of the many ways adults engage in emotionally immature acts. This sort of behavior among adults, however, in no way means that emotions are not important or that they shouldn't be regarded. In fact, our emotions and our ability to control them maturely contribute greatly to a rich and balanced life. In order to have high confidence in life, having high confidence in our emotional state is critical.

In assessing our confidence level in this key life area, we need to evaluate our emotional state from two different perspectives—first, as a sort of "sounding board," meaning that disruptions in any of the other key life areas can result in a disruption in the emotional area, simply because this is where we feel. If I am having difficulty in my relationships, I will feel it in my emotional area. If I am having problems with self-image and my physical key life area, I will feel something of it in my emotional area as well. All of the other key life areas rebound against your emotional state, which is why I put this chapter last—it's vitally important to tune into your emotional heartbeat in order to gain and sustain high levels of confidence in your life.

The second way we need to evaluate our emotional state is as the underlying foundation of all of our other key life areas. If I am suffering from emotional immaturity in anger, for example, this will affect all of my other key life areas. If I am prone to drama and chaos as a preferred emotional state, no area will be left untouched by drama and chaos. Self-awareness is the most important part of evaluating the emotional key life area, in order for us to present to ourselves an accurate picture of where we are in life.

The way we live in this modern society can be so deceptive—we seem to have it all—or at least access to having it all. The truth, however, is that we've cut out of our lives a majority of the things that keep us emotionally healthy, such as strenuous exercise, long-term relationships, involvement with extended family, and meaningful contributions into the lives of others. We rise up, go to work, come home, watch TV or surf the Internet, and go to bed, often disconnected from meaningful interaction.

It can be difficult and painful to develop emotional self-awareness, especially if we've experienced pain or abuse in the past. The human brain has such a complex (and amazingly strong) ability to protect itself, especially from emotional pain, that we can develop coping mechanisms over our lifetimes that we might not even recognize in ourselves. Developing an emotionally based self-awareness is key, not only to gaining and keeping confidence in this life area, but also in determining if we are utilizing unproductive coping mechanisms.

Once we are more clearly aware of our emotional state of being, we can manage those emotions that rise to the surface more often, and we can bring about the changes we might need. Having high confidence in the emotional key life area will allow us to manage our own emotions when they are running high, connect better with others and engage with them in healthy experiences, keep our stress levels low, and keep our lives in general balance.

Our emotional state can be connected to any one of the other key life areas, because we describe all of the other areas in terms of how we "feel" about them. I might "feel" confident or unconfident in the relational area, for example. If I am feeling unconfident in one or more areas, I might be inclined to feel bad in the emotional area as well, simply because it describes my feelings.

Your emotional life ties in closest with your actual state of overall confidence. When I don't feel confident in something, I don't feel emotionally sound, and vice versa. I am in better emotional balance when I feel good spiritually, when I'm in a good relationship, and when my health is good. The emotional area is the least tangible of all the key areas, yet it could be said to be the most powerful one, especially in terms of how it affects our view of our lives.

Emotional maturity (or stability) is the state we should all strive for, but even then, we are likely to have less stable days or time periods. What defines a person as emotionally mature or immature?

An emotionally immature person would be one who struggles with the basics of life—patience (can't delay gratification), forgiveness (holds grudges and blames others), and interactions (manipulates others with feelings). Being in a relationship with an emotionally immature person is exhausting for the other person/people. This person would look like someone who often tries to control others' behavior and opinions, who keeps attention focused on himself, who isn't concerned with how others are treated, and who makes decisions based on what's good for him.

An emotionally mature person exhibits the same maturity in emotions as he does in other aspects of his life—the ability to delay gratification and have patience for outcomes, the ability to forgive himself and others for shortcomings and work for solutions instead of holding grudges, and the seeking of authentic interactions with others, instead of trying to manipulate feelings to get his way. This person would look like someone who can roll with the punches, who can overcome difficulty, who can remain serene and calm under fire, and who can make decisions that benefit everyone involved.

It's critical to understand that negative emotions will occur and that dealing with them is a part of life's journey. Loneliness, grief, sadness, and difficult emotions are all a part of life. One key to having a healthy emotional life is to embrace the emotions that come up inside of us. Have you ever noticed when you are having a good cry that it only hurts when you try to hold it back? "Feeling the feelings" is the only way to process your emotions in a healthy manner.

If we try to ignore our emotions, we just end up with more emotional distress. It actually takes a lot of emotional energy to cover up and hide emotions. We cover our emotions with other emotional problems—in anger problems, overeating or undereating, anxiety and depression, fatigue, alcoholism or workaholism, or some other form of distress. Our goal is to have a rich emotional life that allows us to feel deeply all facets of the emotional range and to build our confidence as a result.

Reasons Why You Might Rate Yourself Low

You might rate yourself with a score of three or lower in the emotional key life area for a variety of reasons. If you recognize the signs of an emotionally immature person in yourself, you might rate yourself low. However, if you recognize the signs and are willing to work on them, you should up your rating. Achieving confidence in the emotional area necessarily means taking a look at some of the ways we behave and justify that behavior and making some changes. All of that takes courage, so if you have an open mind toward becoming healthier, you are on the right path to high confidence.

You might rate yourself low if you feel that most of your day is consumed with negative emotions—turmoil, drama, fear, insecurity, or plain numbness. You might rate yourself low if you are struggling with forgiving someone in your life who has hurt you emotionally. Holding on to anger may make you feel better in the short term, but it is damaging in the long term.

You might question whether your stress load is normal. According to WebMD,[29] how long the stress lasts is the key indicator of its severity. In an article titled "10 Signs of an Ailing Mind," author Colette Bouchez consulted with WebMD experts to put together the following list of symptoms that could indicate a more serious problem:

1. Sleep disturbances more than once or twice a week

2. Dramatic weight fluctuations or changes in eating patterns

3. Unexplained physical symptoms, such as headaches, intestinal troubles, or chronic pain

4. Difficulty managing anger or controlling your temper

5. Compulsive/obsessive behaviors due to excessive worrying, such as rechecking everything multiple times before you leave the house

6. Chronic tiredness and lack of energy or feeling too "beat" to do the things you normally do

7. Memory issues due to preoccupation

8. Shunning social activity or other significant change in behavior

9. Going through the motions in your sex life

10. Mood swings and erratic behavior that your friends have noticed

Each of the above might happen over a long period in single episodes, and that would be normal. But if you can read through that list and check off more than a couple that occur on a regular basis, you probably need to slow down in your life enough to carefully consider your emotional state and the causes behind why you are feeling rattled. If you feel "stuck" and unable to work through the issues, enlist the help of a good friend or consider finding a counselor. Talking to an objective person can shed so much light on complicated issues. A good counselor or therapist doesn't tell you what to think or believe; he or she can help you see yourself and your issues more distinctly, like holding up a mirror for you to look into.

Recommendations to Build Your Confidence

When you experience an emotion that feels out of control, larger than you think it should be, or in some other way unmanageable, look at the situation as an opportunity to figure out another piece of the puzzle that is you. Take time to determine what the emotion is and what other feelings are showing up with it. Take a deep breath and feel the emotion, slow down, and look at it. If you can feel the feeling, you have a better chance at removing the turmoil, and then you can see what's really going on.

When journaling about your emotions, be specific instead of general. The English language is incredibly expressive, and the Internet makes it very easy to find alternative words. Just go to www.dictionary.com and click on the Thesaurus button. Simply type in an emotion you are feeling, and you'll have access to many more specific words. For example, instead of writing that you feel "happy," be more specific as to your exact happiness: excited, glad, joyful, or optimistic. Instead of writing that you feel "angry," be more specific: dejected, unhappy, provoked, or resentful. After you've written it down, allow yourself to completely feel that feeling or emotion. Doing this exercise helps you process the emotions and stop carrying them around like a bag of heavy logs.

Very often, when our emotional state becomes agitated, we actually make the situation worse with our own self-talk. The bully in our heads takes over our inner voice, and we beat ourselves up. As discussed in chapter 3, "Inner Voice," make your inner voice your biggest fan instead of the bully in your head. See yourself as equipped and ready to face the challenges that await you.

Journaling is one of the best activities for dealing with emotional issues. Also, keep a "dream journal" by your bedside, and when you wake up, write down immediately what you remember. If you start paying attention to your dreams in this way, you'll remember more and more of them. Having a better understanding of your subconscious thoughts and dreams will help you create a stronger emotional well-being.

Take time to think through your childhood and adolescence, writing about emotional states and situations that jump out at you. You can often resolve a persistent emotional problem by thinking through the past.

Once again, the Internet provides a wealth of free resources for improving your emotional health and could be a good place to start your journey. Websites such as MentalHealthAmerica.net and the National Institute of Mental Health at NIMH.nih.gov provide fact sheets and other resources for a wide array of emotional health issues, including stress, anxiety, depression, and even tips and tools for staying emotionally healthy.

It's also extremely important to remember that your emotional health can be directly tied to your physical health. One of the best and fastest ways to feel better emotionally is to exercise and get physically active.

Action Plan

As in nearly every aspect of life, becoming aware of the subtle or submerged emotions surging through you can change the dynamics completely. Just like in the financial key life area, you have to figure out where you are emotionally. You can do this by tracking your emotions during the day, week, or month—depending on how much you are struggling in this area. For example, take your "emotional pulse" a few times a day by asking yourself: am I present? Angry? Sad? Anxious? Tracking emotions can provide an insightful view into the real issues, because we can often get lost in time when we feel bad. If you characterize yourself as an emotional wreck, this exercise can help you start to pull out of it.

Another activity that can reduce stress is to create lists. Create a list of the "Top Twenty" actions or responsibilities you have to take care of. When going over the list, focus on the good. Can you delegate any of the tasks to someone else to relieve your stress? Can you move any of the tasks to relieve the pressure you are putting on yourself?

Last, putting into practice the tips and insights we've covered in the other key life areas *will* improve your emotional key life area. As you build relationships and focus on healthy love that promotes personal growth, your emotional state will definitely improve. Exercising and starting to move with physical activity, developing your spiritual outlook, and getting a handle on your finances will definitely improve your emotional key life area. And getting your professional life into a place where you have passion for what you do to earn a paycheck also will improve this area. Take heart! With the encouragement of this book, you can increase your confidence level and live your life with the enthusiasm and health you deserve.

CHAPTER NOTES

29. http://www.webmd.com/mental-health/features/10-signs- ailing-mind, Mental Health Center, Feature Stories. "10 Signs of an Ailing Mind," Colette Bouchez, reviewed by Louise Chang, MD.

"Now is the accepted time, not tomorrow, not some more conve- nient season. It is today that our best work can be done and not some future day or future year. It is today that we fit ourselves for the greater usefulness of tomorrow."

— *W.E.B. Du Bois*

CHAPTER 12

It Is *Today*!

The End Goal

The last sentence of the above quote, "It is today that we fit ourselves …" provides the call to action we all need in order to move forward and grow our confidence level. It is *today* that we do the work necessary. After all, the end goal of this book is to help you achieve a higher confidence, a stable confidence by which you can live out your purpose with intention and fulfillment. Why put this off? Why delay the start of a more confident journey? *Today* is the day that we fit ourselves for tomorrow. It is my hope that we all will be able to exert empowered, informed control over our own lives, rather than being controlled by others or by outside forces or feeling victimized.

It can be difficult to measure whether or not we feel confident, but by breaking down our lives into six key areas, we can sometimes do a better job of isolating our confidence levels within that area. The six key life areas we covered in this book are:

- Relational
- Physical
- Spiritual
- Financial
- Professional
- Emotional

Here is where we will find our true results for our confidence levels. It's here that we will feel and benefit from the effects of stable—and therefore, high—confidence.

Of course, there are plenty of reasons not to take action today. How easy it would be to come to the end of this book and put it back on the shelf, or return it to the friend who lent it to you. But the one thing we cannot stop is the passage of time. One year from now, the only thing we most assuredly know is that it will be a year *later.* What will be different in my life? What will be any different in your life, one year from this very minute, if you don't take action today?

Let's consider what might be at play, keeping us from taking action. First, let's look at the end result. If I take action today, one year from now I will be a more confident and stable individual, healthier, more fit, more in control of my finances, happier in my relationships, more at peace internally, and perhaps pursuing a career I've only dreamed of before. What's not to love about that? So what's in the way? It could be any number of factors, but taken all together, they are likely to fall somewhere around the following three negative factors:

- **Fear**—Fear is the strongest motivator on earth. Psychologists say it's a primal instinct that works to keep us alive and safe. In cases of safety (be afraid of running into a busy street) or survival (be afraid of infectious diseases and take precautions), fear works to protect us. But fear can also work against us if we allow it. I could be feeling afraid, not because following the advice in this book is dangerous, but because I might not know how to be a happier person. I might not know how to function without my dysfunctional crutches. The fear of being something different from what I am now, even if it is better for me, can be a very powerful reason for stopping this process. If you are feeling this fear, recognize it, and don't give up! Reread the book and find a place where you can start and make baby steps.

- **Laziness**—Our lives are relatively easy compared to other time periods in history. We aren't dependent upon hunting our own food daily, and we aren't dying from plagues we can't control. We shop at Kroger and get flu shots. We throw away more food than many families see in a month. This relative ease can also cause us to stay in a sort of "limbo"—a hazy autopilot suburban mambo we do every day, going through the motions of life without actually doing the *work* of living. It's time to throw off that haze and get clear about who we want to be and what we want our lives to look like!

- **Lack of awareness**—Another factor that contributes to the hazy autopilot lifestyle is lack of awareness of any alternatives. However, having now read this book, you can no longer claim lack of awareness. We fool ourselves into thinking that the routine we follow is the same as actually living. The alarm rings, we get up and prepare breakfast, get the kids (if there are any) off to school, go to work, pay the bills, mow the grass, run the errands, feed the dog—often it's not until some tragedy interrupts us, such as a routine visit to the doctor's office revealing cancer or a nagging cough turning into a life-threatening illness, that we take the time to reconsider the path we are on.

It boils down to a very simple question: Do I want the next twenty years of my life to look just like the previous twenty? If we can't break out of our routines, it will just happen. The earth rotates on its axis. Next year is on its way, and when it arrives, the *next* year will then be on its way. Will you be any different a year from right now? Do you want to be?

For worksheets and additional information,
please visit www.tamragaines.com

Printed in the USA
CPSIA information can be obtained
at www.ICGtesting.com
LVHW022317081223
765728LV00031B/553/J

9 781634 135436